翻译中国

中国美食

Translation for China

Topics and Stories About Chinese Food

陈　达　杨天庆 | 编　著
杨天庆 | 审　校

外语教学与研究出版社
FOREIGN LANGUAGE TEACHING AND RESEARCH PRESS
北京 BEIJING

图书在版编目（CIP）数据

翻译中国．中国美食 ：汉文、英文 / 陈达，杨天庆编著．-- 北京 ：外语教学与研究出版社，2022.9
ISBN 978-7-5213-3972-7

Ⅰ．①翻… Ⅱ．①陈… ②杨… Ⅲ．①英语－汉语－对照读物②饮食－文化－中国 Ⅳ．①H319.4：TS

中国版本图书馆 CIP 数据核字（2022）第 180606 号

出 版 人　王　芳
责任编辑　孔乃卓
责任校对　李婉婧
封面设计　水长流文化
出版发行　外语教学与研究出版社
社　　址　北京市西三环北路 19 号（100089）
网　　址　http://www.fltrp.com
印　　刷　北京九州迅驰传媒文化有限公司
开　　本　650×980　1/16
印　　张　12.5
版　　次　2022 年 10 月第 1 版　2022 年 10 月第 1 次印刷
书　　号　ISBN 978-7-5213-3972-7
定　　价　52.90 元

购书咨询：（010）88819926　电子邮箱：club@fltrp.com
外研书店：https://waiyants.tmall.com
凡印刷、装订质量问题，请联系我社印制部
联系电话：（010）61207896　电子邮箱：zhijian@fltrp.com
凡侵权、盗版书籍线索，请联系我社法律事务部
举报电话：（010）88817519　电子邮箱：banquan@fltrp.com
物料号：339720001

序 言

改革开放以来，我国的翻译实践和研究经历了两轮高潮。第一轮高潮即是“翻译世界”。改革开放初期，我们通过翻译，引进和借鉴国外的先进技术和先进管理经验。当时不仅需要掌握外语的人才，翻译人才培养任务也迫在眉睫，因此，很多高等学校增设翻译本科专业。第二轮高潮即是“翻译中国”。在本世纪初，尤其是党的十八大以来，随着中国国力增强和国际影响力加大，中国经济文化等领域迅速走向世界；党的十九大以来，随着中国日益走近世界舞台中央，中国理念、中国智慧、中国方案、中国机遇受到全球关注。新时代、新思想、新使命、新征程，中国同世界关系更加紧密。中国故事，为世界上其他国家谋求发展提供借鉴，为各国共同发展提供启示。中国需要向世界传播自己，世界迫切需要倾听中国的声音。以十九大为起点，中国与世界的互动呈现崭新气象。在中国共产党的领导下，中国理念、中国智慧、中国方案、中国实践在国际舞台上展现出更大的影响力、感召力和塑造力，在人类文明进步、和平发展的大潮中展现出大作为。与此同时，高等学校翻译硕士教育蓬勃发展，为“翻译中国”培养高质量人才，把构建中国国际话语体系任务的重要性提到了前所未有的高度。

“民以食为天”。本著述则从构建“中国美食”国际话语出发，旨在讲述中国美食故事，推广中国美食文化，让外国友人真正体悟到中国博大精深的美食文化和内涵。该著述以英汉形式呈现。著述者发现，目前有一些英文书籍涉及中国饮食文化话题，但尚没有一本常识性、趣味性与学术性皆具的饮食文化英汉读本。为此，著述者结合实际需求，著出本书。

本著述具有以下特点：

第一，含88个话题（方面），涉及中国餐饮文化、菜系文化、小吃调料文化。取材宏富，内容翔实。

第二，通过饮食走遍中国。德州扒鸡、开封桶子鸡、北京烤鸭、南京板鸭、西湖醋鱼、乐山跷脚牛肉、淮南牛肉汤，等等，相信读者会循着这些菜名做一次舌尖上的中国旅行。

第三，通过饮食体味别样的历史。唐代的李密、魏征，宋代的苏东坡，清代的谭宗俊、丁宝桢……是他们赋予了饮食更多的文化底蕴。

第四，中英对照，讲述饮食故事，用英语讲好“中国故事”，弘扬中华民族饮食文化，向世界展示一个生动立体的中国。

本书是国外英语读者了解中国饮食文化的得力助手，也是国内英语学习者的良师益友，同时，它又是中西方文化对比不可或缺的学术研究资料。

陈达于西华大学
杨天庆于四川师范大学
2022年1月16日

目 录
CONTENTS

第一章　餐饮文化
Part One: Food Culture

第二章 菜系文化
Part Two: Chinese Cuisine, a Culture

第三章　小吃调料文化
Part Three: Snacks and Seasonings

第一章
餐饮文化
Part One: Food Culture

1 A Brief Introduction of Chinese Cuisine
中国烹饪略述

Chinese cuisine has a long history. When people first learned to cook, they simply made food over a fire. Or they wrapped food in mud or with leaves, and baked the food over the hot stones under which a fire was burning.

中国烹饪历史悠久。当人类初学做饭之时，仅仅是在火上烤熟食物，或者将食物涂上泥土或用树叶包裹，然后在石块下生火，在炽热的石块上熟化食物。

After the invention of pottery, cooking vessels could be pottery cauldrons, pottery utensils, pottery pots, or others. In those distant ancient times, there were five kinds of grains, but the ancients had different opinions about them. Some people thought the five grains were rice, millet, glutinous millet, wheat, and beans. The vegetables mainly used at that time were bamboo shoots, mustard, radishes, sunflower seeds, garlic, onions, and ginger.

陶瓷出现之后，炊具可能是陶制的鼎、甑、釜或其他陶器。在古时候，有五种谷物，但古人对此说法不一，其中一种说法是稻、黍、稷、麦、菽。当时的蔬菜主要有竹笋、芥菜、萝卜、葵花子、大蒜、洋葱和姜。

Prior to the pre-Qin period, the basic diet of the ancients was maintained at two meals a day. The etiquette of the Han Dynasty stipulated that the emperor had four meals a day, the princes had three meals a day, and the commoners had two meals a day. After the Han Dynasty, two meals a day gradually became three meals per day. In the Song Dynasty, due to the prosperity of economy, the common people really led a life with three meals a day. At this time, if a family was rich, they could eat out in a restaurant, and literati gatherings also took restaurants as a social venue.

先秦之前，古人的基本食制，都维持一日两餐。汉代礼仪规定：天子一日四餐，诸侯一日三餐，平民一日两餐。汉代以后，一日两餐逐渐成为一日三餐。到了宋代，由于经济繁荣，老百姓真正过上了一日三餐的日子。这时候，如果家里有钱，可以下馆子，文人聚会也拿酒楼作为社交场所。

Before the Han Dynasty, only animal fat was used as cooking oil. In the Eastern Han Dynasty, people began to extract oil from plant seeds. During the Qin and Han dynasties, the cooking method of stir-frying became popular among people. There is a record concerning the stir-frying of food in *On the Salt and Iron* written in the Western Han Dynasty.

汉代以前，食用油均为动物油。东汉时期，人们开始从植物籽粒中获取植物油。秦汉时期，炒菜在民间兴起，西汉著述《盐铁论》就有关于炒菜的记载。

During the Wei, Jin, and Northern and Southern Dynasties, China experienced a massive emigration as people of different ethnic groups came and lived together in the same communities in the hinterland of the Central Plains, where they traded food and shared cooking styles. For instance, people from western regions introduced the method of barbecuing food and instant-boiling meat. And people from the southern coastal areas told how to roast goose and cook special seafood.

魏晋南北朝时期，南北交融，不同民族的人们聚集到中原腹地，住在同一个地方。他们交换食物，分享烹饪风格。例如：从西域地区来的人，传入烤肉和涮肉的做法；从南方沿海地区来的人，讲述如何烤鹅和烹制特色海鲜。

During the Tang and Song dynasties, various cuisines flourished. Southern and northen cuisines formed their own systems. In the Southern Song Dynasty, a diet pattern of sweet food in the south and salty food in the north took shape. People focused not only on the taste of food, but also on the color and shape.

唐宋时期，各种菜系繁荣昌盛。南食北食形成各自体系。南宋时期，南甜北咸的格局形成。人们不仅注重食物口感，还重视食物的色泽和形状。

The Ming and Qing dynasties witnessed the continuation of the dietary customs of the Tang and Song dynasties. At the same time, it also had the features of Manchurian and Mongolian cuisines. The dietary life of the Qing Dynasty was rich and active, and the dietetic habits of different regions were also different. Various cuisines formed at that time have been handed down to this day. *The Menus of the Sui Garden* by Yuan Mei from the Qing Dynasty listed many dishes and foods, describing their preparation and analyzing various theories of cooking.

明清时期是唐宋食俗的继续，同时也具有满蒙烹饪特色。清代饮食生活丰富活跃，不同地区有着不同的饮食风俗，而当时形成的各类菜系至今尚存。清代袁枚的《随园食单》列出许多菜肴饭点，详细记述其烹饪方法，并分析各种烹饪理论。

2 Basic Understanding of Chinese Cuisine 中国烹饪知识

Chinese cooking has developed through the centuries. It is one of the delights in China with unique national features. Chinese people value their way of dining very much. As the old saying goes, "Food is the first necessity of the people." Delicious and nutritious food has been regarded as the basic need of ordinary life.

中国烹饪经历了若干世纪，是中国的魅力之一，具有独特的民族特色。有句老话说："民以食为天。"中国人非常重视用餐方式，一直把美味和营养的食物视为日常生活的基本需求。

Eating out is more than just enjoying food; it can be considered a social occasion, a time when families get together, and major leisure activity among friends and businessmen.

人们外出就餐不仅仅是为了进食，可以把它看成是社交需求。这是家庭团聚的时间，是朋友和生意人之间主要的休闲活动。

There are a large number of Chinese restaurants in cities big and small throughout the world. However, you are indeed fortunate to visit China and have an opportunity to try some exquisite local dishes here. You will certainly find a difference in quality, substance, and style in the food prepared in China, compared with the food elsewhere. Many tourists wonder whether it is possible to eat a nutritionally balanced diet while traveling in China. The available ingredients and the styles of cooking vary from region to region, but tourists will always find something to suit their tastes.

世界上大大小小的城市里都有许多中餐馆。不过，能够来中国旅游，并有缘品尝当地的一些美食，确实不虚此行。人们肯定会发现在中国烹饪的食物，其品质、材质、风味皆与在其他地方所吃的食物有些不同。在中国旅游期间，许多游客都想知道是否可以吃到营养均衡的饮食。可用的食材和烹饪风格会因地区不同而有所变化，但游客总能找到适合自己口味的食物。

3 Restaurants in China
中国餐馆

In China, there are many many restaurants. Some of them are small family-run businesses. And some have buffet kitchens, where customers can go to the back of the restaurant to select their vegetables and meats, such as chicken, duck, and fish. Customers may even have a chance to observe how a chef cooks food.

中国有许许多多的餐馆，有些是家庭式小饭馆，有些餐馆厨房是自助式的，顾客可以到餐厅后面自选鸡、鸭、鱼等肉类和蔬菜。顾客甚至还有机会观看厨师烹制食物。

Throughout history, some restaurants won high praise from their customers and became famous because of good service, delicious food and reasonable prices. The names of these restaurants have been handed down from one generation to another. Among the famous names are Quanjude Restaurant in

Beijng, Songhelou Restaurant in Suzhou, and Goubuli Restaurant in Tianjin.

纵观历史，一些餐馆因服务好、食品味美、价格合理而赢得顾客好评，成了名店。这些餐馆品牌一代代地传了下来，其中著名的有北京全聚德、苏州松鹤楼和天津狗不理。

4 Dishes in China 中国菜肴

Many dishes are named after their major ingredients, cooking methods, as well as the names of people and places. Also, fancy and beautiful names are bestowed on many dishes to make them more noticeable to customers. For example, *tianxia diyi xian* (Stir-Fried Clam, Water Chestnut, and Mushrooms) in Jiangsu menu, *qixing yuwan tang* (Fish Ball Soup with Eel, Shrimp, and Pork) in Fujian menu, and *fuqi feipian* (Sliced Beef and Ox Tongue in Chili Sauce) in Sichuan menu. Beautiful dish names create an exciting atmosphere when customers eat their food.

许多菜肴是以主要食材、烹饪方法以及人名、地名来命名的。此外，许多菜肴被赋予了既漂亮又富有想象力的名字，以更吸引顾客。例如，江苏的“天下第一鲜”、福建的“七星鱼丸汤”，以及四川的“夫妻肺片”等。美化的菜名为顾客进餐营造出令人喜悦的氛围。

The key to ordering Chinese dishes is to get a variety and balance of textures, tastes, smells, and colors. Most Chinese will order at least one cold dish, a main dish, a bowl of clear soup, and finish off with a bowl of rice.

点餐的关键不仅要食物品质、口感、味道、颜色多样化，而且还要均衡。多数中国人至少点一道凉菜、一道主菜、一碗清汤，最后再来一碗米饭。

In addition, some delicious snacks are worth trying, as they are cheap and quick to make. The best places to track them down are night markets and lanes in the old areas of the city.

此外，一些美味小吃既便宜，而且制作又快，值得品尝。要品尝小吃，最佳去处是夜市和老城区的小巷。

5 Regional Cuisines in China 中国地方菜系

There are regional differences that offer a diverse range of dishes in Chinese cooking. The most comprehensive and popular ones of these regional "styles," which originated in the North, South, East, and West, belong to roughly four gastronomic areas: Shangdong, Guangdong, Sichuan, and Yangzhou. Although these cuisines are named after provinces or cities, their influence extends far beyond their geographic borders. Each regional recipe has at least one hundred attractive dishes. In addition, there are also some more minor "schools" of regional cuisines.

中国烹饪有地域差异，菜肴种类繁多。在这些地域"风味"菜系里，最全面、最有影响的地方菜系源自东、南、西、北方位，大致上有四大菜系区域，即：山东、广东、四川、扬州。四大菜系虽以省市命名，但其影响所及则远远超出省市地域界限。每个区域的食谱至少有上百种诱人的菜肴。此外，还有一些较小的地方菜系。

Cantonese food in the narrow sense refers to Guangzhou cuisine; in the broad sense, the food includes Chaozhou cuisine and Dongjiang cuisine (also known as Hakka cuisine). The food tends to be lightly cooked and not as spicy as the other three. Many restaurants abroad serve Cantonese cooking, but as you will soon find that the Cantonese food offered abroad is very different from that enjoyed in China.

从狭义上讲，粤菜指的是广府菜，而广义上又包含潮州菜、东江菜（又称客家菜）。与其他三大菜系相比，粤菜相对清淡，不那么辣。许多海外餐馆经营粤菜，但人们很快会发现，海外经营的粤菜与他们在中国吃的很不一样。

In Sichuan province, some dishes are highly spiced and peppery, so it is often said that being hot and spicy is the main characteristics of Sichuan cuisine. Nonetheless, the flavors of Sichuan cuisine can be rather complex. As a popular saying says, "China has food, and Sichuan has flavor." Chefs blend many spices together to create various flavors, including *suanla wei* (hot and sour sauce), *yuxiang wei* (tasty fish-flavored sauce), *mala wei* (hot and spicy sauce), *yanxun wei* (smoked flavor sauce), and so on.

在四川，一些菜既辣又麻，于是人们常说麻辣是川菜的主要特点。尽管如此，川菜味型多样。常言道："食在中国，味在四川。"厨师们将若干调料搭配在一起，调出不同口味，有酸辣味、鱼香味、麻辣味、烟熏味，等等。

Shandong cuisine belongs to the Northern cooking style and should be more accurately described as a representative of the food culture of the Yellow River Basin. Within the realm of northern areas, Beijing, Hebei, Shanxi, and Shaanxi all have their own unique cooking styles. Located on China's eastern seaboard, Shandong cuisine also includes many seafood dishes.

鲁菜属于北方烹饪风格，更确切地说是黄河流域饮食文化的代表。北方各地，如北京、河北、山西、陕西等，都有自己独特的烹饪风格。山东位于东部沿海地区，所以鲁菜还有很多海鲜菜品。

Yangzhou cuisine, also known as Huaiyang cooking, has a wide variety of dishes, with flavors heavily influencing the regions along the middle and lower reaches of the Yangtze River, as well as the middle and lower reaches of the Huaihe River. Yangzhou cuisine tends to be heavier than the Cantonese variety and usually takes a slightly longer time to prepare so that vegetables and meats can absorb the rich sauces.

扬州菜，又称淮扬菜，种类繁多，是长江中下游和淮河中下游的代表风味。与粤菜相比，扬州菜口味偏重，烹饪时间往往稍长，这样肉和蔬菜能够吸收丰富的酱料。

6　Staple Food 主食

The Chinese diet is mainly composed of three parts, namely staple food, non-staple food, and beverage drinks.

中国饮食主要由主食、副食、饮品三部分组成。

The staple food consists of mainly rice and steamed bread. In the long history of agricultural production, grain products have gradually became the staple food, and people mainly rely on them to obtain needed nutrients.

主食主要是米饭和馒头。在漫长的农业生产历史条件下，谷物制品逐渐成为主食，人们主要靠主食取得所需的营养。

Whether you're traveling up a mountain or through a suburb in China, you often find people greeting you with "*Chifan le ma*?", which is literally translated as "Have you eaten rice yet?" This inquiry reveals the significance of food in Chinese culture, and more significantly, the importance of rice in China's history.

在中国，无论你在爬山还是走过市郊，经常会发现人们用“你吃饭了吗？”这句话与你打招呼。此话直译为：“Have you eaten rice yet?”这种询问方式揭示了食物在中国文化中的重要性，尤其是大米在中国历史上的重要性。

Fan may be loosely translated as "grain." In a narrow sense, *fan* means "cooked rice." *Fan* also includes steamed wheat or cornflour bread and noodles. Chinese have the habit of eating more of this food. Grains make up most of one's calorie intake, and an adult may consume two or three bowls of rice or a large bowl of noodles.

“饭”大致可意译成“谷物”。从狭义上讲，“饭”指“煮熟的米饭”。“饭”也包括小麦或玉米馒头和面条。中国人有多食这种食物的习惯，人的卡路里摄入量大部分从谷物中获得，一个成年人可能会吃两三碗米饭或一大碗面条。

7 Non-Staple Food 副食

The non-staple food mainly refers to *cai* (prepared dishes), which is a supplement to the staple food. Materials from nature, which can be used to make dishes, are included in the category of non-staple food. Due to the obvious division of the staple and non-staple food, people usually take the staple food as the main food, supplemented by dishes when eating. Historically, the main food (*fan*) has played a more important role than the non-staple food (*cai*); one of the highest compliments that can be paid to a dish is that it "helps the rice go down" (*xiafan*).

副食主要指做好的菜类食品，是主食的补充食物。大自然中可用于制作菜肴的原料，皆在副食范畴之列。由于主食和副食划分明显，人们在进食时以主食为主，菜肴为辅。从历史上看，主食起着比副食更大的作用，"下饭"一词乃是对菜肴最高的一种褒奖。

In the preparation of the non-staple food, the rule is to use multiple ingredients and several flavors. Vegetables and meat ingredients are usually chopped up into thin, bite-size pieces, which makes knives unnecessary at the dinner table. Beef, for example, may be diced, sliced, shredded, or ground. When the cut beef is mixed with various vegetable ingredients and seasonings, it is usually cooked into individual *cai* dishes with different colors, aromas, flavors, and shapes. Chinese food can also appear whole, like fish and chicken, but they are deeply cooked so that you can easily separate them with chopsticks. These dishes are usually placed at the center of the table to be shared by all.

在烹制菜肴时，原料要丰富，厨师要善于调味。蔬菜及肉类原料时常要切成既薄又小的片（块）状，这样，人们就餐就无须用餐刀了。例如，牛肉可以切丁、切片、切条、剁碎。当切好的牛肉与各种蔬菜和调味料混合在一起时，通常会烹制出独特的菜肴，具有不同的色、香、味、形。中国菜肴也有整形菜，如：鱼、鸡，但都烹得软烂，用筷子便可以很容易分开。通常，这些菜肴放在餐桌中央，供大家分享。

8 *Yin* and *Yang* Featured in Chinese Food 中餐阴阳特征

Traditionally, the Chinese way of eating has been guided by the ancient principle of *yin* and *yang*. Every category of food has its own specific *yin* or *yang* character; meat, vegetables, fruit, nuts, etc. should be consumed in a reasonable combination and balanced amount.

传统上，中国人的饮食方式遵循着古老的阴阳法则：每类食物有其特定的阴阳特性；食用肉、蔬菜、水果、坚果等，都应该合理搭配，食量均衡。

Yin foods are thin, bland, cooling, and low in calories; *yang* foods are greasy, spicy, warming, and high in calorics. Boiling foods makes them *yin*; deep-frying makes them *yang*.

属阴食物呈薄形、温淡、凉性、热量低，属阳食物油腻、辛辣、温热、热量高。煮食为阴，油炸为阳。

Chinese food is expected to be eaten in a certain order. In the Chinese lexicon, the five tastes of food – spicy, bitter, sweet, sour, and salty – are intimately linked with the five primary elements of the Chinese philosophic concept (metal, wood, water, earth, and fire), and with the five primary internal organs of the body.

吃中餐要遵循某种规律。在汉语词汇中，食物的五味，即辛、苦、酸、甘、咸，与中国哲学观念中的五种基本元素（金、木、水、土、火），以及体内五脏有着密切的联系。

The Chinese believe that peppery foods clean the lungs; bitter foods relieve the heart; sour foods refresh and strengthen the liver; sweet foods invigorate the spleen; and salty foods strengthen the kidneys. Some foods have specific effects on the body. Ginseng helps regulate the functions of the glands; seaweed reduces inflammation; lotus root has a significant sedative effect that greatly benefits insomniacs; pickled plums have long been famous for refreshing the stomach and bowels; red beans relieve fatigue and stimulate both the heart and urinary system. Some people think that Chinese food has long been prepared and consumed with more wisdom and more understanding of nutritional and psychological effects of the food.

中国人相信“肺欲辛，心欲苦，肝欲酸，脾欲甘，肾欲咸”。有些食物对身体有特殊效果。人参有助于调节腺体的功能；海藻减少炎症；莲藕有显著的镇静作用，对失眠症患者极有好处；腌渍李子一直以来以能调理肠胃为人所知；红豆可以缓解疲劳，促进心脏和泌尿系统功能。一些人认为，长期以来，中国的食物烹饪与食用更有智慧，更注重饮食的营养和心理效果。

9 The Ways of Chinese Cooking
烹饪方法

The special character of Chinese food derives from the manner of preparation, the method of cooking, the timing, the sauces used, and of course the ingredients.

中餐的特点源于烹饪的准备方式、烹饪方法、烹饪时间、使用的调味汁，当然还有食材。

The first principle of Chinese cooking is to chop, mince, shred, grind, dice, or slice all ingredients into bite-size or paper-thin pieces. The second principle is that the food should be cooked quickly over a very hot fire so that the natural characteristics, including the minerals and vitamins, remain intact. The third principle is to use a wide variety of spices and other taste enhancers, such as coriander, aniseed, sesame, oyster sauce, and soy sauce.

中式烹饪，首要原则是将食材切细、切碎、切条、切丁或切片，使其变得很小或薄如纸片。其二，食物应该在旺火上迅速烹制，这样保持了食物的自然特性，包括矿物质和维生素都不会流失。其三，使用各种调味料、增味剂，如香菜、大茴香、芝麻、蚝油和酱油。

The primary Chinese cooking methods are cold-mix, grilling, deep-frying, shallow-frying, roasting, sautéing, simmering, braising, steaming, and stir-frying. The cutting and ingredients determine how long each dish is cooked. And one of the key arts of Chinese cooking is to be able to judge the right amount of time to achieve the desired taste and appearance.

中餐主要烹饪法有：凉拌、烧烤、油炸、浅炸、烘焙、煸、文火慢炖、焖煮、蒸和爆炒。刀工与食材决定了每道菜的烹饪时间。中国烹饪的主要技巧之一就是能够正确掌握烹饪时间的长短，以达到菜肴理想的口感和外观。

10 The Order in Which Chinese Dishes Are Served 中餐上菜顺序

In ordinary family-style dining, the order of serving varies. In some areas, a meal begins with soup. Next comes a cold-dish appetizer. This is followed by the main entrées and vegetables. White rice is served on the table, accompanying the meal. The last dish is most often fresh fruit.

在普通家庭式用餐中，上菜顺序各不相同。在一些地方，就餐时首先上汤，接下来是一道开胃冷盘，再接下来是主菜和蔬菜。随餐而上的是白米饭，新鲜水果经常在最后端上来。

In a Chinese banquet meal, the cold head-dishes are always served first. These may be assorted hors d'oeuvres, with a variety of meat and vegetables served on the same platter. The first two main courses usually consist of one sauté dish and one deep-fried dish. The next two mid-course dishes are always the spiciest, richest, heaviest dishes of the meal. The following two dishes should consist of one light dish, traditionally fish, and one sweet dish. The last main-course dish is a soup, which signals the end of the banquet. Of course, sometimes rice or noodles are served last. At the end of a banquet, diners often eat a small bowl of rice or noodles.

中餐宴席上，头道菜总是冷盘，有可能是拼盘，即在同一盘上有几种不同的肉和蔬菜。第一、二道主菜，通常是炒菜和油炸食品；接下来的两道菜，总是宴会上味道最辛辣、最浓郁、最油腻的菜肴；再下来的两道菜，应该是清淡的菜肴，按照习俗通常是鱼和甜食；汤是最后一道主菜，这道菜肴预示着宴席即将结束。当然，最后端上桌的有时候是米饭或面条。在宴会结束时，人们会通常吃一小碗米饭或面条。

11 The Situation of Newly Arrived Overseas Tourists Dining in a Chinese Banquet-Style Meal 初到中国的海外游客在中式宴会上用餐的情形

New tourists who are not familiar with Chinese banquet-style meals usually start off by eating too much too soon. At a meal for twelve people, for example, four appetizer dishes will be served at the same time. The new diners almost partake as if they are main-course dishes. Before long, another four dishes are served, some of which are likely to be more filling than the first round. Once again, novice diners take full portions. By the time they finish this round, they are usually full. Then four more dishes — generally famous — are served. Finally, the soup and fruit arrive.

不熟悉中式宴会的海外游客，一开始通常会吃得太多、太快。

例如，在一个招待十二人的宴席上，会同时摆上四道开胃凉菜。初次赴宴的人几乎会把这些菜当成主菜享用。可没过多久，又上来四道菜，其中的一些菜，分量可能比开胃凉菜还要多，用餐者又大吃起来。吃了这几道菜后，他们通常已经饱了。可这时候又上来了四道菜，一般还是有名的菜肴，而且汤和水果最后也端了上来。

The way of serving will definitely surprise these tourists. However, the host will presume that the guests are still hungry and even continue to add new helpings to thcir plates. Traditionally, it is the host's duty to ensure that guests are served and that food is added to their plates during the meal. Besides, the host keeps saying, "Please help yourselves after this." The host seems to overwhelm the guests with food because he/she is simply hospitable. If your host serves you something that you don't like, you may simply leave it uneaten on your plate. During the banquet meal, if you eat too little, it may dismay your host.

这种上菜方式肯定会让这些游客感到意外。然而，宴席主人还以为客人仍然未饱，甚至继续给客人盘里添菜。按照传统习俗，主人有义务照顾好客人，在用餐期间会给客人盘里添菜，还不停地说："吃完后，随便再添。"他们似乎要用食物让客人心满意足，但这是主人好客所致。如果端上来的是你不喜欢的食物，可以不吃，直接留在盘里即可。在宴席上，如果你吃得太少，也可能会使主人不太高兴。

12 Time-Honored Chinese Dining Etiquette
源远流长的中国餐饮礼仪

According to literature records, at least in the Zhou Dynasty, a set of a fairly good system of dietary etiquette had been formed. When Confucius served as libationer in the State of Lu, he highly praised this set of dietary etiquette, which became an important part of the etiquette civilization in the past dynasties.

据文献记载，至少在周代，饮食礼仪已经形成了一套相当完善的制度。孔子在鲁国任祭酒期间，推崇这套饮食礼仪，而这套饮食礼仪也成为历朝礼仪文明的重要部分。

The traditional banqueting etiquette of the ancient Han nationality has its own procedures as follows: A host writes to invite guests. When the banquet arrives, he waits outside the door to welcome the guests. When the guests come, they exchange greetings, and the guests are then shown into a living room, where they sit for a while, drinking tea and eating some pastries. When everyone is present, the guests are shown to their seats at the table. The left side is considered the seat of honor. Opposite the prime seat is a second-class seat. A third-class seat is below the seat of honor, and a fourth-class seat under the second-class seat. After the guests are seated, the host proposes a toast and courteously asks the guests to enjoy the meal. The guests thank their host politely. At mealtime, there is also certain courtesy behavior, such as pouring wine and serving food. First of all, pour wine and serve dishes respectfully to the elderly and chief guest, and then to the host. After the banquet, the guests are shown into the living room, where they sit for a while and are served tea, until they are ready for departure.

古代汉族的传统宴饮礼仪有如下程序：主人折柬相邀，宴会当日迎客于门外。宾客到时，互致问候，然后引入客厅小坐，饮茶吃茶点。客人到齐后，便引导他们入席。以左为上，视为首席，相对首座为二座，首座之下为三座，二座之下为四座。客人入座后，由主人敬酒让菜，客人以礼相谢。席间斟酒上菜也有一定的讲究：先敬长者和主宾，最后才是主人。宴饮结束，引导客人入客厅小坐，上茶，直至辞别。

In modern times, the life-style has changed greatly, but the traditional etiquette for banquets is still preserved in our culture. Of course, the etiquette varies from region to region. With the continuous exchange of Chinese and Western food culture, Chinese food is more and more favored by foreigners.

在现代社会里，人们的生活方式发生了很大的变化，但是传统宴饮礼仪在我们的文化中仍然保留着。当然，饮食礼仪因地区而异。随着中西饮食文化的不断交流，中餐越来越受到外国人的青睐。

13 Guidelines for Dining with a Chinese Family 与中国家庭一起用餐的礼节

General speaking, there are two styles of Chinese meals — family style and banquet style. The family style, in which everyone helps himself or herself from a number of shared dishes, can be found both in homes and in restaurants.

一般来说，中餐有两种模式：家庭模式和宴会模式。无论是在家还是在餐馆，都可以看到家庭模式的用餐方式，即每人从若干共享菜肴里自行取用。

Dining in Chinese homes usually doesn't need much courtesy. The first time you are invited, bring an inexpensive present; if the family has children, bring small gifts for them as well. Upon entering the home, you will be introduced to family members with whom you are not acquainted. In some places, if your principal host is the husband, the wife might be in the kitchen; if your principal host is the wife, the husband might be the one in the kitchen. Within the last hour or so before the meal begins, the preparation of a Chinese meal can be so frenzied and lively that the cook is likely to be out of sight most of the time. If he or she has a seat at the table, it will be the one closest to the kitchen. Maybe you are accustomed to waiting until everyone is seated and everything is served, but this expectation cannot be met when a large meal is being prepared in a Chinese home. Don't insist on waiting until the cook arrives.

中国家庭用餐一般无须太多讲究。如果你首次应邀出席家宴，就带一份不算昂贵的礼物；如果这家人有孩子的话，也要带些小礼物。一进门，主人会向你介绍你不认识的家庭成员。在一些地方，如果丈夫是宴请人的话，妻子可能会待在厨房里；如果妻子是宴请人的话，丈夫可能是待在厨房里的人。大约开饭前的最后一小时，中餐准备工作可能会忙得不可开交，大部分时间很可能看不见厨师的影儿。如果餐桌旁有厨师坐的地方，那就是距离厨房最近的那个座位。也许你习惯等到所有人坐好并让菜上齐后再进餐，但当中式家宴是一顿大餐时，这种期待恐怕会落空的，没有必要等到做饭的人到后再进餐。

Besides, you should make appreciative comments about the food and hospitality, but be prepared, too, for the host will apologize for various inadequacies. You should graciously reply that the meal is plentiful and delicious.

此外，你还应该对食物和款待表示谢意，感谢之情应溢于言表。不过，宴请人会为各种不足之处表示歉意，对此你也要有心理准备，礼貌地回答道："这顿饭菜很丰盛，味道可口。"

During any Chinese meal, guests should make appreciative remarks about at least some of the dishes on the table and about the general quality of the event. Remarks of this kind should be repeated at the end of the affair, too, especially by those who sit far away from the host(s) during the meal.

食用中餐时，客人至少应该点评餐桌上的一些菜肴和整个酒席的服务质量，言语里要充满赞赏之词。那些离主人较远的客人，尤其在宴会结束时应该重复说这些话。

14 The Seating Custom of a Formal Dinner 宴会座位习俗

Seating arrangements are very important at meetings with Chinese, including meals — whether or not they are officially hosted. In the case of formal dinners, the host and chief guest usually sit on opposite sides of the table, facing each other. The other guests are seated to the left and right of the chief guest in descending order of rank or importance.

与中国人会晤时，座次安排尤其重要，其中包括正式或非正式的用餐招待。在正式宴会上，主人和主宾通常会面对面地坐在餐桌两边。其他宾客按照职务或重要程度，由高到低依次坐在主宾左右两侧。

If you are the only host, the seat on your right must be reserved for the chief guest; the seat on your left is for the second-chief guest. If an interpreter is needed, he/she usually sits on the right side of the chief guest. Other guests are seated to the right of the chief guest in descending order of rank or importance. Foreign guests who are not familiar with the Chinese custom of seating should not rush to sit down. They should wait for the host to indicate where they are to be seated.

如果是单主陪同的话，那么宴请人的右边座位一定是留给主宾的，左边座位为第二副主宾。如果需要译员的话，一般安排在主宾右侧。其他客人按照地位或重要程度，由高到低依次坐在主宾右边。凡是不熟悉中方座次习俗的外国宾客，切莫匆忙就座，而需等待宴请人安排座次。

15 Different Types of the Feasts of the Confucius Mansion 孔府宴的种类

Confucius said, "One eats no rice but is of the finest quality, nor meat but is finely minced." The culinary culture in the hometown of Confucius has a long history. "A trip to Qufu would not have been successful without a feast of the Confucius Mansion." This saying is the high praise by Chinese and foreign tourists for the cuisine of the Confucius Mansion. In addition, it is also a unique name card of the cultural industry in Confucius' hometown.

孔子曰："食不厌精，脍不厌细。"孔子故里的饮食文化有着悠久的历史。孔府菜是孔子故里文化产业的一张独特名片，"不食孔府宴，枉来曲阜游"，是中外游客对孔府菜的高度赞誉。

The Feasts of the Confucius Mansion are divided into different types, such as birthday feast, flower feast, happiness feast, greeting-guest feast, and home-style dinner. In those days, these were high-class banquets specially prepared in the Confucius Mansion when honorary guests visited the mansion, or when the person of the mansion inherited the rank of nobility or received an official post, or when a birth-date, a wedding or a funeral occurred. One may well say that they are a complete collection of Chinese feasts.

孔府宴种类不同，如寿宴、花宴、喜宴、迎宾宴、家常宴，是当年孔府接待贵宾、袭爵上任、生辰、婚丧时特备的高级宴席，可谓集中国宴席之大全。

Birthday feast: In the Confucius Mansion there exists a special book, which records the birthdays of Yan Sheng Gong (the hereditary title for the eldest son in the Confucius family) holders, the holders' wives, the sons, the daughters, as well as the birthdays of their relatives and key staff in the mansion. In those days, when a birthday came, there would be a celebration feast. As time went by, this kind of dinner parties became a birthday feast. The name of each dish for the feast has its own hidden meaning, such as the Good Luck and Long Life, the Amazing Longevity and the Envy of Ducks, the Longevity Fish, and so on. Among them, the Yipin Birthday Peach is considered to be the first dish at the birthday feast of the Confucius Mansion.

寿宴：孔府专门备有册簿，记载衍圣公及夫人、公子、小姐，以及至亲等主要成员的生辰。每当生日到来时，都要设宴庆祝。周而复始，便形成了寿宴。寿宴的菜肴名称各有寓意，如“福寿绵长”“寿惊鸭羡”“长寿鱼”等。而“一品寿桃”是孔府寿宴中的第一珍肴。

Flower feast: It was a kind of banquet held when Yan Sheng Gong holders or their son had his wedding or their daughter was married out. The names of the dishes for the feast sound both appropriate and elegant, such as the Peach Blossom and Shrimps, the Mandarin Chicken, etc.

花宴：这是衍圣公和公子婚礼及小姐出嫁时所举办的一种宴席。菜肴名称既贴切又雅致，如“桃花虾仁”“鸳鸯鸡”等。

Happiness feast: It was another kind of banquet held when an official position or a hereditary peerage was conferred, or the birth of a son or other happy events were congratulated. The names of the dishes for the feast sound beautiful and auspicious, such as Four-Happiness Meatballs.

喜庆宴：凡孔府内遇有受封、袭封、得子等喜庆之事，都要办宴祝贺，其菜名多美好、吉祥之意，如“四喜丸子”。

The greeting-guest feast: It refers to a high-class banquet, which was held when an emperor or royal ministers came for a visit. The feast featured delicacies from land and sea and had the highest formality.

迎宾宴：指的是迎接圣驾或款待王公大臣等高级官员时所举办的宴席。席面上有山珍海味等，礼节规格最高。

Home-style dinner: It refers to a large or special meal prepared to entertain relatives and friends. The menu often varied with the season.

家常宴：指的是为招待亲友所用的宴席，菜品常随季节而变换。

16 The Manchu-Han Full Banquet, a Well-Known Chinese Feast 中华著名大宴：满汉全席

The Manchu-Han Full Banquet is mainly composed of the cuisines from Northeast China, Shandong, Beijing, Jiangsu and Zhejiang. Originated in the Qing Dynasty, it is a well-known Chinese feast, which combines the essence of the cuisines from the Manchu and Han ethnic groups.

满汉全席以东北、山东、北京、江浙菜为主。它兴起于清代，汇集了满族与汉族菜点精华，是中华著名大宴。

Before the Qing army entered the Shanhai Pass, Manchurian royal banquets were very simple. At a common feast, diners would lay animal skins in the open place, where everyone sat together eating. Usually, the cooked food was hot pot in which pork, beef, and mutton were stewed. As for the state banquet attended by the emperor, there were a dozen or only a few dozens of tables. The food was also beef, mutton, and pork; and diners cut the meat into small pieces and ate them with carry-on knives. After the Qing army entered the Shanhai Pass, the Manchurian royal diet soon became rich. It was updated on the basis of the original traditional Manchurian cuisine and absorbed the features of the southern-style cooking mainly from Jiangsu and Zhejiang, as well as the northern-style cooking known as Shandong cuisine. In the beginning, the court separated the Han banquet from the Manchu one. According to *The Code of the Qing Dynasty*, during the reign of Emperor Kangxi the Manchu banquets prepared by the Guanglu Department (an organ in charge of royal feasts and court meals) were usually divided into six grades, while the Han banquet fell into five categories, namely, the first-class, second-class and third-class formal dinners, as well as the high-level special meal and intermediate special meal. Initially, the formal feast started with a Manchu banquet, and then a Han banquet followed. Later, people gradually merged the two different kinds of the meals, hence the name of the Manchu-Han Full Banquet.

清入关之前，满族宫廷宴席非常简单。在普通宴会上，用餐者会把兽皮铺在露天里，大家围坐在一起就餐。通常，所做的食物就是火锅，里面炖煮的有猪肉、牛羊肉等。至于皇帝出席的正式宴席，也就设置十几张或几十张桌子，食物也是牛肉、羊肉、猪肉等，而食客们用随身携带的刀把肉切成小块，然后再吃。清入关后，宫廷饮食很快变得丰富起来。在原有的满族传统饮食的基础上出现了新的变化，吸取了以苏浙菜为主的南方菜系和以鲁菜为主的北方菜系的特点。当初，宫廷的满汉宴席是分开的。据《大清会典》记载，康熙年间，光禄寺承办的满席通常分为六等；承办的汉席，则分一、二、三等，以及上席、中席，共五类。最初宴请嘉宾时，先吃满席，再上汉席。后来，人们遂将两席的肴馔融于一体，于是就有了“满汉全席”之名。

Traditionally, the Manchu-Han Full Banquet has exquisite dishes. Before a banquet begins, two pairs of incense, tea and plates are set out. On the table are four kinds of fresh fruit, four kinds of dried fruit, as well as four kinds of ornamental fruit and four kinds of candied fruit. After everyone takes his/her seat at the banquet, cold dishes, hot stir-fried dishes, large bowls of food and sweet food are served in turn. There are 196 dishes of cold dishes, meat dishes and hot dishes, as well as 124 kinds of desserts, cakes and sweets. In addition, a complete set of longevity utensils is used. Coupled with silverware, this type of utensils shows wealth and brilliance. During the banquet, musicians play ancient music, while the guests enjoy the delicious food and the elegant legacy.

传统的满汉全席菜点精美。入席前，先上两对香、茶水、手碟；桌面上有四鲜果、四干果、四看果和四蜜饯；入席后，冷盘、热炒菜、大菜、甜食依次上桌。冷、荤、热肴共计一百九十六品，还有点心茶食一百二十四品。此外，宴席用的是全套万寿餐具，并配以银器，这种餐具显得富贵华丽。席间，乐师奏古乐伴宴，客人享受着美食和典雅遗风。

17 The Banquet for Thousand Elders Held in the Qing Dynasty 千叟宴在清朝

Words *qiansou* mean "Thousand Elders." The Qiansou Banquet was one of the large-sized royal feasts in the Qing Dynasty. It was initiated in the Kangxi years and held four times. These banquets were substantial; their scene was magnificent; in history, it was unique.

汉字"千叟"指的是"千位老年人"。千叟宴始于康熙年间，共举办了四次，是清朝宫廷的大型御宴之一。这些宴会极其丰盛，场面极大，在历史上也绝无仅有。

On the occasion of the 60th birthday in 1713, Emperor Kangxi held the first Qiansou Banquet in the Garden of Everlasting Spring. The first banquet invited old people aged over 65 to the capital city from all over the country to celebrate the emperor's birthday.

1713年，康熙皇帝六十寿诞，他在畅春园举办了第一次千叟宴。首次千叟宴请了全国各地65岁以上的老人到京城为皇帝祝寿。

In the Kangxi sixty-first year (1722), Emperor Kangxi was 69 years old. In order to celebrate his 70th birthday, he held a second Qiansou Banquet in front of the Palace of Celestial Purity on the second day of the first lunar month to entertain eight banners' civil and military ministers, officers, as well as officials who resigned or retired from official posts. A total of 680 people over the age of 65 took part in the banquet. Many princes and royals came out to offer drinks and distribute food to the elders. On the fifth day of the lunar month, another banquet was held for 340 elderly Han Chinese aged over 65.

康熙六十一年（1722），康熙帝年届69岁，为了庆祝自己70岁生日，正月初二日，他在乾清宫前举办了第二次千叟宴，招待八旗文武大臣、官员及致仕官员。赴宴者680人，年纪在65岁以上。诸王及宗室成员都来向老人们劝饮，分发食物。初五日，又举行了一次宴请340位65岁以上汉族老人的宴会。

On the sixth day of the first lunar month in the Qianlong fiftieth year (1785), Emperor Qianlong held a Qiansou Banquet for the elders to show his infinite royal graciousness. It took place in the Palace of Celestial Purity, a spectacular scene with more than 800 tables. More than 3,000 participants were aged over 60 years old. They included princes, royals of the Manchu nobility, ministers of civil and military affairs, and officials who resigned or retired from posts and who were granted civil or military ranks. This banquet showcased the royal grandeur: the royal chefs not only elaborately prepared the Manchu-Han Full Banquet, but also provided alcoholic beverages from royal tributes.

乾隆五十年（1785）正月初六日，乾隆帝举办了千叟宴，以示皇恩浩荡。宴会在乾清宫举办，场面大，计800多席。约有3,000余名年过60岁的人共聚一堂。来者有亲王贝勒、文武大臣官员、致仕大臣官员、受封文武官员等。这场宴会尽显皇家气派，不但有御厨精心制作的满汉全席，还有作为皇家贡品的酒水。

On the fourth day of the first lunar month in the Jiaqing first year (1796), Qianlong held a grand banquet, the last feast for the elders in the Qing Dynasty. That year, 86-year-old Qianlong abdicated in favor of his son Yongyan who ascended the throne and became Emperor Jiaqing. This banquet was held in the Hall of Imperial Supremacy, the reception room of the Palace of Tranquil

Longevity, where the banquet was attended by 3,056 elders. When the banquet began, the royal music was played. Accompanied by Emperor Jiaqing, the emperor's father Qianlong ascended to the special chair in the hall. At the banquet, the princes, dukes, first-rank ministers and other over-90-year-old elders were invited to the front of the special chair, where Qianlong personally gave them the royal wine. At the same time, he ordered his sons, grandsons, great-grandsons, and great-great-grandsons to serve wine to the princes, the dukes, and the ministers there. Meanwhile, the palace guards served wine to the attendees who sat at tables outside the hall. During the banquet, the participants improvised poems, and a total of 3,497 poems were collected after the banquet.

嘉庆元年（1796）正月初四，乾隆举办了盛大的宴会，这也是清朝最后一次千叟宴。时年，乾隆86岁，已经退位，颙琰即位为嘉庆皇帝。此次宴会地点在宁寿宫的皇极殿，来的老人共计3,056名。宴会开始，皇家音乐奏响，在嘉庆皇帝的侍奉下，太上皇升上殿内宝座。席间，王公、一品大臣、90岁以上的老叟受邀到御座前，乾隆亲自赐给御酒。他又命皇子、皇孙、皇曾孙、皇玄孙，给殿内王公大臣行酒；皇宫侍卫负责给殿外的参宴者行酒。参宴者即席赋诗，宴会后结集的诗作共计3,497首。

18 The History of the Tan's Home-Style Cuisine 谭家菜的历史

The Tan's Home-Style Cuisine originated from Tan Zongjun's family. So far, it has existed for more than one hundred years.

谭家菜是谭宗浚的家人创立的。迄今为止，谭家菜已经有百余年的历史了。

In the Tongzhi thirteenth year of the Qing Dynasty (1874), Tan Zongjun of Nanhai in Guangdong arrived in Beijing, where he served as an official in the Imperial Academy. Later, he worked as an educational inspector in Sichuan, and then as a deputy examiner in the regions south of the Yangtze River. Tan Zongjun loved delicate and tasty food all his life. At the same time, he was very hospitable and liked to entertain his friends with dinners or banquets. The chefs he employed were all well-known cooks from Beijing, so the dishes featured a combination of Cantonese and Beijing cooking styles. What's more, Tan Zongjun and his son's persistent pursuit of culinary practice and food tastes led them to master cooking skills and even develop their own styles.

同治十三年（1874），广东南海人谭宗浚入京翰林院为官，后督学四川，再后又充任江南副考官。谭宗浚一生酷爱珍馐美味，亦好客酬友。他聘请的厨师皆是京师名厨，其菜肴集粤菜和京菜于一体。更重要的是，由于谭宗浚与儿子对烹饪制作和风味的不懈追求，他们很好地掌握了烹饪技艺，自成一派。

In 1909, Tan Zongjun's son Tan Zhuanqing returned to Beijing. There, due to his family's delicious food and his family's social status, he often invited distinguished guests to his home for dinner, and his hospitality thus promoted the development of the Tan's Home-Style Cuisine. At the time, it was in vogue for Beijing officials to attend the Tan's home-style dinners or banquets. However, the Tan's family financial situation unfortunately deteriorated, so Tan had to start catering business with his home-style menu in order to subsidize his family. Gradually, the Tan's Home-Style Cuisine became one of the best-known family-style cuisines in the country.

1909年，谭宗浚之子谭瑑青返京。因为谭府的“谭家菜”味极醇美和谭府的社会地位，谭瑑青经常邀请贵宾到府邸饮馔，他的好客由此促进了谭家菜的发展。一时间，京师官僚假谭府宴客成为时尚。不幸的是，谭府经济每况愈下，谭瑑青不得不用私家菜开业经营，以补贴入不敷出的谭府。谭家菜渐渐地成为全国最著名的私家菜之一。

In the 1930s, the Tan's Home-Style Cuisine became even more famous. At that time, celebrities or dignitaries from all walks of life in politics, military, commerce, and culture often entertained guests or friends with the Tan's home-style dishes, so as to show off their wealth or glory. As for table reservations for the Tan's home-style dishes, people would book half a month in advance. Those who visited Beijing would feel good and happy if they could have a chance to taste these dishes.

到了20世纪30年代，谭家菜更为有名。当时，政界、军界、商界、文化界的名流要人常用“谭家菜”宴客，借以显耀其富贵和荣光。人们通常提前半月预订谭家菜。如果到京师之人有机会品尝到这些菜肴，也会感到非常高兴。

Traditionally, if customers wanted to taste the Tan's home-cooked dishes, they have to go to Tan's home, but the members from the Tan's family would not stand outside to greet them. Customers usually filled and emptied their cups of wine three times before a waiter started to bring food to the table. Usually, the dishes were the Nest of Cliff Swallows in Light Soup, the Abalone Braised in Soy Sauce, etc. Then, there were many other dishes, and the last of course was sweet and salty pastries. When the dinner was over, everyone got up and walked into a reception room, where they ate fruit and drank tea.

按惯例，如果顾客想吃谭家菜，就得去谭府，但谭府家人是不会站在府外相迎的。顾客酒过三巡，服务员开始上菜，通常是清汤燕菜、红烧鲍鱼等。然后，还有若干道菜肴，最后一道是甜咸糕点。众人吃完谭家菜，便站起来，走进会客室，在那里饮茶，吃水果。

In those days, the Tan's Home-Style Cuisine was a fashionable specialty. Therefore, there was a popular saying: "In the theater circle, there is no one who does not learn singing from the Tan (Tan Jiaotian); in the circle of food and beverages, there is no one who does not love the Tan (the Tan's Home-Style Cuisine)."

当时，"谭家菜"成了时尚招牌菜，故此曾流传有"戏界无腔不学谭（谭叫天），食界无口不夸谭（谭家菜）"这两句话。

19 The Legend of the Eight Big Bowls
八大碗的传说

The Eight Big Bowls are traditional Chinese specialties, which are cooked differently in different regions. These include the Eight Big Bowls in Zhengding, the Eight Big Bowls in Tengzhou, the Eight Big Bowls in Anhui, the Eight Big Bowls in Linqing, and others.

八大碗为中国传统特色饮食，各地八大碗做法不尽相同，有正定八大碗、滕州八大碗、安徽八大碗、临清八大碗等等。

Legend has it that the Eight Immortals annoyed the Dragon King when they crossed the sea. The immortals engaged the king, and the battle lasted for quite some time. When they could hardly win, they retreated to the beach for a rest. By then, they felt hungry and went away in different directions to look for food. Unexpectedly, because of no human habitation around the beach, they all came back disappointed, except Cao Guojiu.

相传，八仙过海时，惹怒了龙王。八仙与龙王开战，打斗持续了很长时间，但几乎难以取胜，于是他们便退到海滩歇息。这时，八仙都感到饥饿，便四处寻找食物。没想到，由于海滩周围荒无人烟，除了曹国舅外，其余的皆失望而归。

Cao Guojiu himself rode on clouds to the hinterland. There, disguised as a peasant, he entered a farm house, where a pleasant smell greeted him. He saw eight people sitting around a square table and drinking their fill, with the bowls of tempting food being served.

曹国舅一人腾云驾雾，去了内地。他乔装打扮成一名农夫，走进一家农舍，里面香味扑鼻。他看见方桌旁有八人围坐，畅怀痛饮，桌上是一碗碗诱人的食物。

Cao Guojiu thought, "I was once the king's uncle on the king's mother side and tasted all kinds of dishes from the palace, but I have never seen food like this here. Why don't I eat first?" However, it occurred to him that all the other immortals were still hungry. How could he enjoy the food on his own? So, Cao Guojiu took away seven bowls of dishes. Then, he remembered that the immortal He Xiangu was a vegetarian, so he took away a bowl of vegetarian food, which consisted of green vegetables and tofu. Totally, there were eight bowls. Before his departure, Cao Guojiu left a message saying, "Guojiu has borrowed eight bowls from you for the immortals, and I will repay you for your kindness in the future."

曹国舅寻思道："我原乃朝廷国舅，尝过宫廷各种菜肴，却未见过这样的农家菜肴，我何不先吃呢？"然而，他想起众仙友还在挨饿，自己怎能独享呢？于是，便拿走了七样菜肴，又想起仙姑不食荤，便带走了一碗青菜豆腐素菜，共计八大碗，并留言："国舅为众仙借菜八碗，日后定当图报。"

These eight bowls of food smelt delicious, and the Eight Immortals devoured them eagerly. After that, they felt refreshed and fought the Dragon King again until they won a complete victory. Later, the *fangzhuo* (square table) was renamed *baxian zhuo* (table for eight immortals or square table for eight people). And the food eaten by the eight immortals was called *shi bacai,* which means *ba lengdie* (Eight Cold Dishes) and *ba dawan cai* (Eight Big Bowls). Currently, the updated names are still in use.

这八碗菜肴很香，八仙狼吞虎咽地吃了下去。之后，他们精神倍增，再战龙王，大获全胜。后来，人们把"方桌"改称"八仙桌"，八仙吃的食物则改称"食八菜"，其意为"八冷碟"和"八大碗菜"，更改后的名称一直沿用至今。

20 The Origin of the Bouyei Eight Big Bowls
布依八大碗的由来

The Bouyei Eight Big Bowls are the best dishes for Bouyei ethnic group to entertain guests. In southwestern Guizhou, the first view of the Wanfeng Resort is the First Bouyei Village, where the Bouyei Eight Bowls can be said to be the best choice for locals and tourists alike. The eight bowls of dishes include the Stewed Trotters with Golden Soybeans, the Braised Pork in Brown Sauce with Cubes of Tofu, the Braised Pig Skin, the Crispy Meat with Bean or Sweet Potato Noodles, the Stewed Spare Ribs with Radish, the Steamed Pumpkin, and the Colorful Glutinous Rice.

布依八大碗是布依族招待宾客的最好菜肴。黔西南万峰景区第一观为布依第一寨，那里的八大碗可谓当地人和游客喜爱的上等佳肴。八大碗是猪脚炖金豆米、红烧肉炖豆腐果、炖猪皮、酥肉粉条、排骨炖萝卜、素南瓜、素豆腐、花糯米饭。

Legend has it that in the Ming Dynasty, Emperor Zhu Yuanzhang dispatched Wang Dengke to lead his troops to Yunnan. Wang's men went on a long expedition. When they reached Xingyi, more than half of his troops were dead or wounded because of an unhealthy, unpleasant smell in the jungles on the Yunnan-Guizhou Plateau. Meanwhile, most of their daily necessities were lost.

相传，明朝皇帝朱元璋派王登科领军征伐云南。当时，军队长途远征，由于云贵高原山林多瘴气，官兵到达兴义府时，死伤过半，日常用具等都已丢失殆尽。

When they arrived at Shangpo Hill, Wang Dengke saw in front of them a vast plain surrounded by mountains. So he ordered his soldiers to be stationed there and build fortifications and barracks.

这时，他们到达上坡岗，王登科见此地四周群山环抱，中间有块坝子却一马平川，便命令兵丁修筑工事、营盘。

By then, the troops had only pots and jars left. Due to a shortage of kitchen utensils, they produced more earthen jars, pots, and bowls with local firing methods. The soldiers used these big bowls to hold food when eating. As time went by, the locals developed the habit of serving dishes in big bowls, hence the Bouyei Eight Big Bowls.

那时候，随军的只剩下一些坛坛罐罐。炊具缺乏，他们用土法烧制了一些陶制坛罐和锅碗瓢盆。士兵们吃饭时，就用这些缸钵或海碗来盛饭菜，久而久之，当地人养成了用大碗盛菜的习俗，由此衍生出“布依八大碗”。

21 The Emergence of the Sidewalk Snack Booths 大排档的产生

The term *paidang* (a roadside food stand) comes from Guangdong. Its roots may be traced back to the corrupt practice of ancient times. According to the court menu of the Southern Song Dynasty, even the royal family members did not eat meat every day. Therefore, court service officials often used their own money to treat the emperor, nobles, or ministers to dinner. Soon, it became common practice. At that time, the way that court service officials took turns serving food was called *paidang*.

“排档”一词来自广东，其根源可以追溯到古代的一些腐败做法。根据南宋宫廷的菜单，即便是皇室成员也并不是每天都有肉吃。于是，朝廷侍官常常自掏腰包，请皇帝、贵族和大臣吃饭，这很快形成一种风气。当时朝廷侍官排队轮流请客的方式被称为“排当”。

In the beginning, court service officials paid out of their own pockets or claimed back their bills elsewhere. In the years when Li Zong reigned, their expenses could be paid back by the central government or financial institutions at various levels. At that time, Chen Zongli, a local military commander in Guangdong, was transferred to work as a senior assistant in the General Military Headquarters in the capital, where he witnessed such “corruption.”

起初，朝廷侍官自掏腰包，或找地方报销。到了南宋理宗统治年间，朝廷侍官可以拿账单到中央或各级财政部门报销。当时，广东经略使陈宗礼调任京城枢密院参知政事，他在那里看到这种“腐败”现象。

He said that people of lower ranks treated their superiors to dinner, only for the purpose of reaping some profit from their bill's reimbursement or seeking for special favors or assistance. As a result, Chen submitted a written statement to the relevant authorities, discussing a possible ban on the *paidang*. However, he received no response, and the practice of the *paidang* continued unchanged.

他说，下级请上级吃饭，无非为了报销时捞点油水，或者是拉拢关系，寻求特殊帮扶。因此，陈宗礼上书相关部门，探讨禁止“排当”的可能性。然而，上书石沉大海，而“排当”的做法仍然没有改变。

Later, the term *paidang* began to be widely used to refer to the small, open-air, roadside food businesses. Each place had simple facilities, such as a number of tables and chairs, and provided inexpensive food to meet the demand of common people. Locals in Guangdong called this place *dang* or *dangkou*, which was later renamed *paidang*. As for the name of big *paidang*, it is derived from the Food and Beverage License issued in the early time in Hong Kong. At that time, such licenses appeared to be larger in size than those of ordinary small food stands, and they were asked to be displayed in a visible place. As a result, a stand with a large-sized license was gradually called Big Paidang (the Sidewalk Snack Booths).

后来，“排当”一词泛指露天街边的餐饮摊点。每个摊点设施简单，提供一些桌椅，并提供大众消费得起的便宜食物。广东人称之为“档”或“档口”，后又改名为“排档”。至于“大牌档”之名，则源于早期香港颁发的餐饮经营牌照。当时，这种牌照比发给普通小档口的看起来要大，并须放在显眼之处。于是，拥有这种大牌照的档口，逐渐称为“大牌档”或“大排档”。

22 Etiquette of Toasting (1)
敬酒礼仪（1）

Whether you dine at a restaurant or someone's home, liquor or beer is commonly served, and a selection of soft drinks is also available. Wine may be served for the purpose of toasting, but you may toast with anything, even a soft drink. Official toast in China is *ganbei*, which literally means "empty your glass," but in English the equivalent is "bottoms up." Generally, guests are expected to *ganbei* only for the first time. Subsequent toasts – and there may be many of them – can be sipped.

无论在餐馆或在他人家里用餐，招待的常有白酒或啤酒，还有一些可供选择的饮料。白酒可能是用来敬酒的，但你可以用其他酒水替代，甚至饮料也可以。在中国，祝酒的正式称呼叫“干杯”，其字意是“喝完杯中酒”，相当于英语中的“bottoms up”。一般来说，主人希望客人能够喝下首杯酒，接下来的敬酒可能有若干次，但每次只需喝一小口即可。

Generally, the host makes a speech first, the chief guest responds and then everyone begins participating in toasts. Other individuals on the host's side normally take the lead in toasting guests who are seated closest to them.

一般而言，主人先致辞，主宾答谢，然后大家开始敬酒。陪客的人通常率先向离自己最近的宾客敬酒。

At a formal banquet, when there are more than one table, the host, after his opening remarks, will usually go to each additional table to clink the glasses of each individual at that table and then drink a toast to them. The chief guest is expected to follow this same manner after he responds, leaving his/her table to clink glasses with those at other tables.

在正式宴请上，如果不止一张餐桌的话，主人在开场白之后，常常会走到每一张餐桌前，与每桌人碰杯敬酒。主宾在答谢之后也要这么做，离开自己的餐桌，去与其他桌的人碰杯。

If the host or some other banquet member proposes a "sip" toast, and anyone in the banquet does a "bottoms up," it is considered a special politeness for everyone to follow suit. The toast may be to deepen friendship and improve cooperation or relations.

如果主人或其他宴会成员提议举杯浅酌，而宴会上有人仰杯而尽，此举视为一种特殊礼节，要他人照此效仿。干杯的目的可能是为加深友谊、增进合作，或改善关系等等。

23 Etiquette of Toasting (2)
敬酒礼仪（2）

Toasting is necessary at banquets. It may be awkward or considered impolite if you refuse to drink at a dinner party entertained by a Chinese host, unless you have a good reason such as high blood pressure, an upset stomach, etc. If you really can't drink, you can fill your glass with tea instead. Joining the toast with water, tea, or a soft drink is acceptable.

敬酒在招待宴会上是不可缺少的。在中国，如果在东道主举办的宴会上拒绝喝酒的话，可能会显得尴尬，或有失礼貌，除非事出有因，如高血压、胃不舒服等等。如果真的不能喝酒的话，可在酒杯里倒入茶水代替。用茶、水，或不含酒精饮料来敬酒是可以的。

Another way to limit the amount of alcohol that you drink during toasts is not to fill your cup or glass to the top. Using this strategy will allow you to get more involved in *ganbei*. If you happen to be the object of attention of numerous toasts, it is perfectly acceptable, moreover, to raise your glass to your lips and sip the wine lightly.

敬酒时，还有一种限制饮酒量的方法，即不要斟满酒杯。使用这种办法可以参与多次敬酒干杯。如果碰巧成为若干敬酒的对象，不妨将酒杯举到唇边，轻轻抿一小口，这是完全容许的。

24 Features of Chopsticks 筷子文化

At the beginning of a Chinese meal, it is a signal for everyone to begin eating when the host picks up his/her chopsticks. If you haven't mastered using chopsticks before coming to China, you probably will by the time you leave.

中餐开始时，如果主人拿起筷子的话，这就表示大家可以用餐了。如果有人来中国前还不会使用筷子，那么当他离开之时可能就会了。

Chopsticks have been used in China for thousands of years. In some restaurants, sometimes the waiter will bring out the silverware for foreign guests. However, when you attempt to master the use of chopsticks, hosts will show indefinite patience with you, and you will be surprised at the speed of your progress.

筷子在中国已经使用了几千年了。在一些餐厅，服务人员有时候会为外国客人提供刀、叉等餐具。然而，当有人努力要学会如何使用筷子时，主人们通常对学习者极有耐心，而且学习者会对自己进步的速度甚感惊讶。

Chopsticks are made of a variety of materials ranging from plain wood, lacquered wood, bamboo, and ebony. Chopsticks can be square or round in shape. Generally, chopsticks are round at one end and square at the other. If one end of the chopsticks is round and the other end is square, then the former symbolizes the heaven and the latter symbolizes the earth. When holding chopsticks, the index finger and the thumb are at the top, the ring and little fingers are below, and the middle finger is in the middle. This gesture symbolizes heaven, earth, and human beings.

筷子可由各种材料制成，有一般木材做的筷子、漆筷、竹筷和乌木筷。筷子形状或方或圆。一般来说，如果筷子一端为圆，另一端为方，那么圆是天的象征，方是地的象征。拿筷子时，拇指和食指在上，无名指和小指在下，中指在中间，这种手势象征着天、地、人。

Table manners deserve studying. One thing you should never do is to stick your chopsticks vertically into a bowlful of rice. This is considered a bad omen as it resembles an incense stick that is burning at a Chinese funeral. Another thing you should never do is to beat a bowl or a pot with your chopsticks. Some people think that this could be a reminder that beggars would tap on their bowls or pots with their chopsticks when asking for food.

餐桌礼仪值得了解。其中一件事是不能做的，就是不能把筷子竖立着插在一碗米饭里。这种做法被认为是不吉利的，因为竖立着的筷子类似于中国葬礼上燃烧着的香烛。另一件事也是不能做的，就是不能用筷子敲打碗盆：有些人认为这可能会让人想起乞丐用筷子敲打碗盆讨饭的举动。

第二章
菜系文化
Part Two: Chinese Cuisine, a Culture

25 Gongbao Chicken, a Famous Traditional Classic Dish
传统经典名菜：宫保鸡丁

Gongbao Chicken (Stir-Fried Chicken with Peanuts) is a famous traditional dish. There are several stories concerning the origin of Gongbao Chicken. Most people believe that this dish falls into the category of Sichuan cuisine. According to legend, it was invented by locals in Sichuan, and later further developed by Ding Baozhen who once served as Governor-General of Sichuan in the Qing Dynasty.

宫保鸡丁是传统名菜，来历有若干说法。多数人认为这道菜属川菜菜品。相传，这道菜是由四川当地人创始的，后来由清代当时任四川总督的丁宝桢加以改进发展。

However, locals in Shandong disagree, saying that this dish was invented by Ding Baozhen when he served as Provincial Governor of Shandong. For this reason, Gongbao Chicken is also believed to be a recipe of Shandong cuisine.

然而，山东当地人却不这么认为，说这道菜是丁宝桢任山东巡抚时发明的。因此，宫保鸡丁也被认为是鲁菜的一道菜肴。

People from Beijing see it another way. Gongbao Chicken was one of the palace dishes of the Qing Dynasty, a tradition that might lead one to think of it as a palace-style dish.

北京人则有另一种看法：宫保鸡丁是清朝宫廷的一道菜肴。这可能会让人认为这道菜是宫廷风格的菜肴。

At last, locals in Guizhou disagree with the above points of view. One story says that Guizhou was Ding Baozhen's hometown. Once, he returned to Guizhou for a short visit to his parents. When he arrived home, his relatives and friends gave him a feast. Among the feast courses was a dish of fried cubed chicken with green pepper, which deeply satisfied him. He immediately asked what the dish was called. Someone attempted to please him and said, "This dish is cooked especially for Your Excellency. Its name is Gongbao Chicken." "Gongbao" was Ding's honorary title. According to this story, locals in Guizhou consider Gong Bao Chicken to be a local dish in their hometown.

最后，贵州当地人不同意上述观点。一则故事说，贵州是丁宝桢的家乡。一次，他回贵州作短暂逗留，探望父母。归家后，亲朋好友备好酒席款待他。席间，有一道青椒炒鸡丁令丁宝桢深感满意。他立刻问这道菜的菜名。有人取悦他道："这道菜是特意为您烹制的，取名'宫保鸡丁'。""宫保"是丁氏的名誉官衔。据此，贵州当地人认为宫保鸡丁是本地的一道地方菜。

After that, Ding went back to his office. He soon hired the man to cook for his family because the banquet meal impressed him so much. At home, he added peanuts and Chinese prickly ash to this dish. From then on, whenever Ding hosted a banquet, he would arrange his chef to make Gongbao Chicken with Peanuts to entertain his guests. Later, his descendants used chilies instead of Chinese prickly ash to produce the Sichuan-Styled Gongbao Chicken.

之后，丁宝桢回到自己的官府。他很快就雇用这个厨师为家人做饭，那顿宴席令丁宝桢印象深刻。在家里，他还给这道菜加了花生和花椒。从此，每当丁宝桢设宴待客时，他就安排厨师烹制宫保鸡丁。后来，丁宝桢的后人用辣椒替代花椒，做出了川味宫保鸡丁。

In the period between the end of the Qing Dynasty and the beginning of the Republic of China, Sichuan cuisine spread to major cities across the country, and at the same time Gongbao Chicken became famous both at home and abroad as one of the most famous special dishes of Sichuan cuisine.

清末民初，川菜走向了全国各大城市。与此同时，宫保鸡丁也闻名国内外，成为川菜中一道最著名的特色菜肴。

26 The Origin of Dezhou Braised Chicken
德州扒鸡的故事

During the period between the end of the Yuan Dynasty and the beginning of the Ming Dynasty, Dezhou became a channel of nine provinces to Beijing transporting grain to supply the capital or meet military demands. There, the economy was booming, and braised chicken was on sale at markets. With the development of economy, the braised chicken in Dezhou in those days not only appeared on dining tables of restaurants, but also was sold by people carrying baskets with braised chicken in them. Around canal docks and post stations or near the city's official offices, here and there were old men who carried baskets crying braised chicken for sale. The skin of the braised chicken appeared red, the smell is aromatic, and the meat tasted tender and delicious.

元末明初，由于漕运繁忙，德州通达九省，那里的经济呈现繁荣之势，市面上有烧鸡出售。随着经济的发展，这时的德州烧鸡不仅在饭店供应，还有挎着篮子叫卖烧鸡的。运河码头、驿站周围，或城内官衙附近，到处都是提着篮子叫卖烧鸡的老人。这种烧鸡色红，香气扑鼻，肉嫩可口。

In the thirty-first Kangxi year of the Qing Dynasty (1692), there was a man named Jia Jiancai who ran a braised-chicken store on the main street outside the West-Gate of Dezhou City. His retail business was good because this street led to the canal docks.

清康熙三十一年（1692），有个叫贾建才的人，在德州城西门外大街上经营着一间烧鸡铺。因这条街通往运河码头，小买卖做得还不错。

One day, Jia Jiancai, the store owner, had to go out because of an urgent matter. So he asked one of his servants to control the fire on the stove for a while. However, no sooner had the store owner gone than the servant fell asleep by the cooking range.

一天，店主贾建才因急事要外出，便嘱咐店小二压好火。然而，店主前脚一走，小伙计就在锅灶旁睡着了。

When he woke up, he found that the chickens were overcooked over the fire and he was at a loss what to do next. Just then, the store owner came back. He tried to get the chickens out and sold them in the store. Unexpectedly, the chickens smelt good and attracted many passers-by to buy them. Some of them took a bite and praised profusely. They said, “Not only is the meat extremely tender, but it smells good. And even its bones are crunchy and tasty to chew on.” After that, the store owner focused on cooking braised chicken. And this gave rise to the original recipe of this dish: boil chickens over a high heat, simmer them over a low heat, and carefully control the heat of the fire.

当他醒来时，发现鸡都炖过火了，不知道怎么办才好。这时候，掌柜回来了，他试着把鸡捞出来，拿到店面上去卖。没想到，鸡香诱人，吸引了很多过路行人购买。有的行人尝了一口，赞不绝口地说：“不只是肉烂味香，就连骨头嚼起来也是又酥又香。”从那之后，店主专注于与扒鸡相关的烹饪方法，于是便产生了扒鸡的原始做法，即大火煮，小火焖，管好火炉。

The Jia-style chicken thus became famous, so the regular customers suggested giving a name to the braised chicken. The store owner couldn’t think out of a good name for a moment. After a while, it occurred to him that in the street lived an old scholar whose surname was Ma. He thought that the old scholar could give it a good name.

贾家鸡由此出名了，老主顾们建议给这道菜取个名字。贾掌柜一时想不出来。又过了些日子，他忽然想起临街有个马老秀才，认为他准能给取个好名字。

So, the store owner took out two steaming hot chickens out of the pot, wrapped them up in lotus leaves and hurried to Ma’s house. Scholar Ma tasted the chicken and asked how it was cooked. Then, he chanted smoothly, “As the hot chicken is shaken, its flesh separates from its bones; at the same time, an exotic smell unexpectedly assails to the nostrils, prompting the old man to hold out five fingers; and as the meat goes into his mouth, its aroma remains in his teeth for ages." After chanting, the old scholar uttered impulsively, "What braised chicken with the meat separated from the bones!"

于是，掌柜从锅里拿出两只热气腾腾的鸡，用荷叶包好，快步走到老马家。秀才尝了尝鸡，问了问做法，便顺口吟出："热中一抖骨肉分，异香扑鼻竟袭人。惹得老夫伸五指，入口齿馨长留津。"诗成吟罢，脱口而出："好一个五香脱骨扒鸡呀！"

The store owner sold his braised chicken at the Lantern Festival the next year; his sale was very good, and its reputation increasingly grew from then on.

第二年元宵节，店主卖扒鸡，销路很好，自此名声大振。

27 Tongzi Chicken, a Specialty in Kaifeng
开封名吃：桶子鸡

Tongzi Chicken is one of the most famous dishes found in Kaifeng. One cannot talk about it without first talking about Ma Yu Xing, a century-old store in Kaifeng founded by Ma Yongcen. The famous Ma family had its origins in Yunnan but moved to Jinling when Wu Sangui led his army into Yunnan in 1659. After settling in Jinling, they opened a company called Chun Hui Tang.

桶子鸡是开封名吃之一。说到桶子鸡，首先要说的是开封的百年老店"马豫兴"。马豫兴的创始人是马永岑。马家原在云南，家势显赫。清朝顺治年间，吴三桂率军入滇，马家随后迁至金陵，并在那里开设了商号"春晖堂"。

During the Xianfeng years, Jinling fell into chaos due to the war between the Taiping army and the Qing troops. The Ma

Family headed by Ma Yongcen came to Kaifeng.

咸丰年间，由于太平军和清军之间的征战，金陵陷入混乱之中，马家在马永岑的带领下来到了开封。

In Kaifeng, Ma Yongcen ran a firm called Yu Sheng Yong that sold mainly foods. At the same time, he found that the Central Plains were rich in chicken resources, so he produced a new kind of chicken meat from local hens with the same method he used to cook the Nanjing ducks. This chicken, called Tongzi Chicken (chicken in the shape of a bucket), looks bright yellow and tastes saltedly delicious. The more Tongzi Chicken you chew, the better it tastes.

在开封，马永岑经营了一家叫“豫盛永”的商号，主要销售食货。与此同时，马永岑发现中原地区有许多鸡，他就用加工南京鸭的方法，用当地母鸡烹制出一种新型的鸡肉。这种鸡叫“桶子鸡”，色泽鲜黄，咸香味，越嚼越香。

At that time, Tongzi Chicken was very popular. In the third Tongzhi year (1864), Ma Yongcen opened a new store. Today, many chicken stores in Kaifeng can make Tongzi chicken, as Ma Yongcen did before.

当时，桶子鸡很受欢迎。同治三年（1864），马永岑开了新店。如今，开封许多售卖鸡制品的店铺，像马永岑那样皆会制作桶子鸡。

28 The Origin of the Beggar's Chicken
叫花鸡的来历

The Beggar's Chicken is also known as the Simmered Chicken. It is a famous dish although its name doesn't sound nice.

叫花鸡又称“煨鸡”。虽然名字不太好听，却是一道名菜。

Legend has it that in the late Ming and early Qing dynasties, there was a beggar at the foot of Yushan Mountain in Changshu. One day, the beggar got a chicken by chance, but he had no cooking utensils and seasonings. He thought about it for a long time. Suddenly, a good idea occurred to him. He slaughtered the chicken and removed its internal organs. Then he covered the feathered chicken with mud. He picked up some dead sticks, made a fire with them and roasted the chicken over a small fire. When the mud became dry and cracked, he knocked off the mud shell, and the chicken feathers also fell off with the shell. By then, the chicken smelt good, and it tasted tender and delicious. The beggar was overjoyed and started eating it eagerly.

相传明末清初，常熟虞山底下有一个乞丐。一天，这个乞丐偶然得到一只鸡，但他没有炊具和调料。他苦思良久，忽然想到了一个好主意。他宰了鸡后除去内脏，连鸡毛一起裹上泥巴，然后捡了一些枯树枝生火，将鸡放在小火中煨烤。等到泥干裂后，他敲掉泥壳，鸡毛也随着泥壳脱落下来。这时的鸡很香，肉又嫩又好吃。乞丐大喜，迫不及待地吃了起来。

Just at that time, Qian Muzhai, a Ming-dynasty great scholar who lived in seclusion in Yushan, happened to pass by. A unique smell greeted his nose. Looking through the leaves, he saw the beggar devouring the chicken, so he sent his home servant to ask how to roast it. Meanwhile, he asked the servant to bring back to him a piece of the chicken.

就在这时，隐居在虞山的明朝大学士钱牧斋正好路过此地，奇异的香味扑鼻而来。透过树叶，他看到乞丐正在大吃鸡肉。于是，他便叫家仆上前询问烤鸡的做法。同时，他还让仆人给他取一块鸡肉回来。

After tasting it, the great scholar found that the chicken had a very special flavor. When he got home, he told his servant to roast the chicken with some seasonings, as the beggar did. A few days later, Liu Rushi came from Songjiang to Qian's home for a blind date. The great scholar held a feast to host her. One of the dishes was the roast chicken. The chicken smelt good, its skin was crispy, and its meat was well roasted. He said to Liu with a beaming smile, "What do you think of the Yushan taste?" Liu pointed at the chicken with her chopsticks and said, "I would rather eat Yushan chicken all my life than Songjiang fish for a day." When she knew how the roast chicken was made, she named it "the Beggar's Chicken."

大学士品尝后，发觉鸡味确实独特。回到家后，他吩咐家仆用乞丐的做法稍加调料烤鸡。几日后，柳如是从松江来钱府相亲。大学士设宴款待她，其中一道菜就是烤鸡：那鸡又香，皮又酥，肉还烤得好。大学士满面笑容地问柳如是："虞山的风味如何？"柳如是用筷子指着烤鸡说道："宁食终身虞山鸡，不吃一日松江鱼。"她问明缘由后，便将这道菜命名为"叫花鸡"。

29 Time-Honored Peking Roast Duck
历史悠久的北京烤鸭

The history of the roast duck can be traced back to the Yuan Dynasty when it was listed as one of the royal dishes in the book named *The Complete Recipes for Dishes and Beverages* written by Hu Sihui, an imperial physician and nutritionist. Details regarding the cooking process were also described in this cookbook.

烤鸭的历史可以追溯到元朝。当时饮膳太医忽思慧的《饮膳正要》就把烤鸭列为宫廷菜，这本烹饪专著也记载了这道菜的相关烹饪过程与细节。

In the early 15th century, when the Ming Dynasty relocated its capital from Nanjing to Beijing, the roast duck remained one of the famous dishes on the court menu. According to local historical records, the earliest Peking duck restaurant was the Old Bianyifang Restaurant, which opened during the Jiajing period. The restaurant roasted ducks in a unique way. First of all, the walls of the ovens in the restaurant were heated with sorghum stalks. Ducks were then placed inside the ovens and hung from hooks on the oven ceiling. The wood below burnt steadily, and the heat given off by the walls slowly roasted the hanging ducks. The duck roasted in this way is crispy and golden-brown in appearance; its meat is tender and tasty.

15世纪初，明王朝从南京迁都北京，烤鸭依然是宫廷菜单上的名菜之一。根据当地历史记载，北京最早的烤鸭店是嘉靖年间开业的老便宜坊。老便宜坊烤鸭方法极具特色。首先，用高粱秆加热坊里的炉壁，再把鸭子放进烤炉，并用炉顶挂钩钩住鸭子；下面的柴火不断燃烧，炉壁散发出热量，慢慢烤着悬挂的鸭子。用这种方法烤制的鸭子外表酥脆，呈金褐色，肉质软嫩可口。

During the Qianlong years, the roast duck was a delicacy favored by the upper classes. According to *The Recipes of the Suiyuan Garden*, a famous cookbook written by the poet and gourmet Yuan Mei, "Roast ducks are produced by hooking up ducklings and roasting them. The chefs in Inspector Feng's family excel in preparing this dish."

乾隆年间，烤鸭是勋戚贵族的佳肴之一。诗人、美食家袁枚的名作《随园食单》说："用雏鸭上叉烧之。冯家厨最精。"

To meet the growing demand for roast ducks and take

advantage of its good reputation, many restaurants opened under the name of Bianyifang. In 1926, in Beijing there were nine roast duck restaurants that carried this name. In the late 1960s, Bianyifang Restaurant changed its name to Chongwenmen Roast Duck Restaurant, but its original name was resumed in 1979. Traditionally, there are more than 20 duck dishes on the menu including "the Four Delicacies": duck tongue, duck feet, duck pancreas, and duck breast.

为了满足人们对烤鸭日益增长的需求，并利用其良好声誉，许多餐馆皆以"便宜坊"的名义开业。1926年，北京有九家烤鸭店就以此命名。20世纪60年代末，便宜坊更名为崇文门烤鸭店，但1979年又恢复了原名，其鸭类传统菜肴有二十多种，包括"鸭四宝"（鸭舌、鸭掌、鸭胰、鸭脯）。

30 The Origin of Nanjing Salted Pressed Duck 南京板鸭的来历

Nanjing Salted Pressed Duck, a famous specialty at home and abroad, is made in a unique way. The ducks are autumn fat ducks from northern Anhui, northern Jiangsu, and the surrounding areas of Nanjing. After they are slaughtered, the ducks are washed and marinated with seasonings. More than a dozen of hours later, the flavors of seasonings and salt have seeped into their flesh and bones. Then, the salted ducks are hung out to dry. As the ducks are soaked in a marinade, many of the ducks are stacked in rows in jars. The jars are covered with bamboo lids, and stones are placed on the top of the lids to press the ducks into the shape of a plate object, so the ducks are called *banya* (Salted Pressed Duck).

南京板鸭是驰名中外的风味食品，制作方法独特，鸭子选自皖北、苏北及南京周围地区的秋季肥鸭。鸭子宰杀后洗净，再用佐料腌制。十几个小时后，佐料盐味就沁入鸭肉鸭骨之中。然后，咸鸭便被挂出晾干。在腌制之时，很多鸭子一排排码放在缸里，缸上用竹盖盖住，并在上面压上石头，将鸭子压成板状型，故称“板鸭”。

According to legend, during the Southern and Northern Dynasties when Emperor Liang Wudi came to the throne, he established his capital city in Jiankang (present-day Nanjing). In 548, General Hou Jing rose in rebellion. He besieged Taicheng, the seat of Liang's court government and the imperial palace in Nanjing. The fighting was so intense that Liang's soldiers did not even have time to eat.

相传南北朝时期，梁武帝即位，建都城于建康（即今南京）。公元548年，大将侯景起兵叛乱，围困台城，当时的朝廷台省和皇宫所在地。战斗十分激烈，梁朝士兵无暇顾及饭食。

At that time, it was mid-autumn, and fat ducks were sold in the market. So women in Taicheng washed fat ducks and cooked them with seasonings, salt, and other sauces. The cooked ducks were then wrapped in lotus leaves and sent to the battlefield. As many soldiers and officers were involved in the battle to defend Taicheng, numerous cooked ducks were tightly bundled together and brought to the place where the soldiers and officers were. These men untied the bundles of ducks, boiled the ducks in water, and then ate them.

当时，正值中秋，肥鸭上市。于是，台城内的妇女们便把肥鸭洗净，佐以香料、盐、酱等烹制，然后把做好的鸭子用荷叶包裹好，送到前线。将士们都在防守台城，很多鸭子被捆扎起来，抬到官兵所在地。将士们打开成捆的鸭子，用水一煮，便能食用了。

Later, in order to commemorate the battle, the Taicheng

people called these pressed ducks *banya* (Salted Pressed Duck). Its recipe has been passed down from generation to generation, and the method of its preparation is getting better and better.

后来，为了纪念这场战役，台城百姓便把压扁的鸭子称为“板鸭”，其制作方法代代相传，而且越做越好。

31 Emperor Qianlong and the Steamed Duck with Dried Vegetables
干菜鸭子与乾隆皇帝

The Steamed Duck with Dried Vegetables is a traditional dish in Jiande, Zhejiang Province. It is said that its origin relates to the Southern Inspection Tour by Emperor Qianlong of the Qing Dynasty.

干菜鸭子是浙江建德的一道传统菜肴，据说起源与清朝乾隆皇帝下江南有关。

When Emperor Qianlong passed through the regions along the lower reaches of the Yangtze River, he noticed many ducks swimming in rivers and lakes. Once, when it was almost lunchtime, the emperor came to a roadside inn for food. He asked the inn chef to single out a duck to cook. Quickly, the chef slaughtered a duck, but did not have enough time to remove some of its feathers.

在乾隆皇帝游历长江下游地区时，发现河湖里有许多戏水的鸭子。有一天，快到午餐时间了，乾隆帝便来到路边一家小店用餐。他让厨师挑选一只鸭子来烹制。仓促间，厨师宰了一只鸭子，但却没有足够的时间去掉一些鸭毛。

An idea occurred to the chef. He cooked the duck well. Then

he took out the duck bones, placed the duck flat on a food steamer, and sprinkled it with dried vegetables and other seasonings. These dry vegetables, black in color, covered the duck skin, so the emperor could not see the stubborn feathers. The duck had been steamed over a hot fire. Then, the chef turned the duck over and poured a mild sauce on it. He presented the duck to the emperor. After eating, the emperor praised it greatly.

厨师想到了一个办法。他煮熟鸭子，取出鸭骨，将鸭子平放在蒸笼上，并在鸭子身上撒上梅干菜和其他佐料。这些干菜呈黑色，包裹着鸭皮，这样乾隆帝就看不见难以处理的羽毛。鸭子旺火蒸后，厨师翻过鸭身，在上面浇上淡汁，然后献给乾隆帝。乾隆食用后，大加赞许。

Before long, the emperor returned to the capital, where he still remembered the steamed duck eaten in Yanzhou Prefecture of Jiande. He then made the imperial chef cook the duck. However, the duck made by the chef displeased the emperor. The imperial chef became very worried, and he hurried to Yanzhou, where he visited the small inn for advice on cooking the ducks. The news spread quickly that the imperial chef had come here to learn how to cook the Steamed Duck with Dried Vegetables, so people came to the inn to taste it. Gradually, this dish became well known in the local region.

不久，乾隆皇帝返回京城，他还记得在建德严州府吃过的蒸鸭。于是，他让御厨烹制鸭子。可是，御厨做的鸭子却令他不悦。御厨急了，便赶到严州，向小店厨师请教烹制鸭子的方法。京城御厨来此学习干菜鸭子的消息不胫而走，于是人们便来到小店品尝干菜鸭子。天长日久，干菜鸭子在这个地区声名大噪。

32 The Legend and Evolution of the Poached Fish in Sweet Vinegar Sauce 西湖醋鱼的传说与演变

The Poached Fish in Sweet Vinegar Sauce is a famous traditional dish in Hangzhou. The fish is the grass carp from the West Lake. This dish is said to have a long history, dating back to the Song Dynasty. At that time, there was a family that included an elder brother, his wife, and a younger brother. Unfortunately, the elder brother was killed by a local bully, leaving his wife and younger brother behind. The younger brother and the elder sister-in-law tried to revenge for the elder brother, but failed again and again. Then, the younger brother had to take refuge elsewhere. Before he left, his elder sister-in-law cooked a sweet and sour fish for him. Later, the younger brother succeeded in the imperial exam for an official rank, and the bully was finally punished. Legend has it that the Poached Fish in Sweet Vinegar Sauce was also known as A Hereditary Treasure Between the Younger Brother and Elder Sister-in-Law.

西湖醋鱼是杭州的一道传统名菜，鱼为西湖的草鱼。据说这道菜历史悠久，可以追溯到宋朝。当时有一家人，家里有一长兄、长兄媳妇和长兄的弟弟。不幸的是，哥哥被当地恶霸杀害，留下了他的妻子和弟弟。叔嫂二人想为他报仇，却屡遭失败。小叔子不得不到外地避难。临行前，嫂嫂为他烹制这道糖醋鱼。后来小叔子考取了功名，恶霸最终受到惩治。所以，西湖醋鱼又叫“叔嫂传珍”。

Some people say that the Poached Fish in Sweet Vinegar Sauce evolved from Sister Song's Fish Soup (Fish Soup with Ham and Mushrooms). According to *The Old Stories of Martial Arts*, Sister Song was a famous chef. Once, Gao Zong, the Emperor of the

Song Dynasty, visited the West Lake by a dragon boat and tasted the fish soup cooked by her. Since then, Sister Song's Fish Soup remained very popular. After the innovation by unknown experienced chefs, this dish later evolved into two famous dishes, namely the Poached Fish in Sweet Vinegar Sauce and Sister Song's Fish Soup.

有人说，西湖醋鱼是由“宋嫂鱼羹”演变而来的。根据《武林旧事》记载，宋嫂是一位著名厨师。宋高宗乘龙舟游西湖时曾尝其鱼羹。从那以后，宋嫂鱼羹一直很受欢迎。后来，这道菜经过不知名但有经验的厨师创新后演变成两道名菜：西湖醋鱼和宋嫂鱼羹。

But in fact, Sister Song's Fish Soup probably evolved from the Hot and Sour Fish of the Qing Dynasty. *The Menus of the Sui Garden* by Yuan Mei lists the recipe of the Hot and Sour Fish. It says, "Cut live a black carp into large chunks, deep-fry these pieces in oil and then sprinkle them with soy sauce, vinegar, and wine. The more the soup is, the better. When it is ready to serve, remove the pot from the heat immediately. This is a famous dish in Wuliuju Restaurant on the West Lake in Hangzhou."

其实，宋嫂鱼羹应该是由清代的醋熘鱼演变而来的。袁枚《随园食单》上就有醋熘鱼的记载：“用活青鱼切大块，油灼之，加酱、醋、酒喷之，汤多为妙。俟熟即速起锅。此物杭州西湖上五柳居有名。”

Later, in Hangzhou there was a well-known restaurant called Louwailou which made the Poached Fish in Sweet Vinegar Sauce. In addition, Yu Yue, a famous scholar of the Qing Dynasty, contributed a lot to the fame of this dish. He cooked this dish in a way that absorbed the cooked method of Sister Song's Fish Soup, as well as the fish cooked by Deqing people. When his secret recipe came to light, the Poached Fish in Sweet Vinegar Sauce became a unique dish in Hangzhou.

后来，杭州一家叫“楼外楼”的名店烹制出了西湖醋鱼。此外，清代著名学者俞樾在让西湖醋鱼名扬四海方面也起了重要作用。他烹制的这道菜，兼取宋嫂鱼羹和德清人烹鱼的方法。当秘方流传出后，西湖醋鱼遂成杭州一绝。

33 Stories About the Boiled Fish with Pickled Chinese Cabbage 酸菜鱼的典故

Story One 传说一

The Boiled Fish with Pickled Chinese Cabbage is a soup made with fresh fish and pickled green cabbage. Because the pickled green cabbage tastes sour, it obtains the name *suancai yu* (the Boiled Fish with Pickled Chinese Cabbage). In early winter, the locals in Sichuan like to preserve green cabbage in a large earthen jar and make family-styled pickled vegetables. These vegetables can be taken out of the jar as needed. In most cases, they are used to make soup with chicken, duck, fish, or pork.

酸菜鱼是用鲜鱼加泡青菜做成的汤。因泡青菜味酸，故名“酸菜鱼”。初冬，四川当地人喜欢在大坛里储存青菜，腌渍出家庭风味的酸菜。这些酸菜随用随取，多与鸡、鸭、鱼、猪肉一起做汤菜。

Story Two 传说二

The Boiled Fish with Pickled Chinese Cabbage originated from the Zhouyu Inn in Jinfu of Jiangjin in Chongqing. In the mid-1980s, the inn mainly served this dish, which was very popular with local diners. The Zhouyu Inn received many apprentices. After the completion of their learning, they left the inn and opened their own eateries elsewhere, and therefore the

Boiled Fish with Pickled Chinese Cabbage could be found in many places.

酸菜鱼始创于重庆江津津福的周渝食店。20世纪80年代中期，该店主要经营酸菜鱼，这道菜深受当地食客的欢迎。因此，周渝食店就有了不少徒弟。这些徒弟学成之后，便离开此地到别处开店，酸菜鱼也随之流传到四面八方。

Story Three 传说三

In Bishan of Chongqing there was an old man who was good at fishing. One day, he caught some fish. He went home and gave the fish to his wife. By accident, she cooked the fish in the pickled cabbage soup. The old man tasted it, and it was very delicious. He praised it every time he met other locals, and thus the Boiled Fish with Pickled Chinese Cabbage became famous.

重庆璧山有一位老人，擅长钓鱼。一天，他钓到几尾鱼。回家后，他把鱼给了老伴。老伴误将鱼放入酸菜汤中烹煮。老人尝了尝，鲜美可口。于是，他逢人就夸，“酸菜鱼”也由此而出名。

Story Four 传说四

In Bishan there is a river called Binan River. The river flows through Laifeng Town, where there are plenty of fresh fish, and many chefs are good at cooking fish. At the end of a bridge, there was a small eatery named *xianyu mei* (Fresh and Delicious Fish). Over the door on the lintel hung its name label, which not only displayed its name, but also solicited its business. The eatery invented a dish called *shuizhu yu* (Fried and Boiled Fish with Garlic Sprouts and Celery) and it was very popular for years. Later, it made *suancai yu* (the Boiled Fish with Pickled Chinese Cabbage). The taste was so unique that many other restaurants in Chongqing followed suit.

在重庆璧山，有一条河，名璧南河。这条河穿过来凤镇，此地鲜鱼产量多，众多厨师擅长烹鱼。在一座桥头尽头，有一家小食店，取名“鲜鱼美”。小食店门楣上挂着牌匾，既作店名，还可以招揽生意。小食店推出了水煮鱼，多年来一直很受欢迎。后来，又推出酸菜鱼，风味独特，重庆许多餐馆纷纷效仿。

Story Five 传说五

The Boiled Fish with Pickled Chinese Cabbage originated from cooking on fishing boats in Jiangjin of Chongqing. It is said that local fishermen would sell big fish for money and take the remaining small fish to local farmers in exchange of pickled cabbage. The fishermen would stew pickled cabbage and fresh fish in the same pot. Surprisingly, the food tasted really delicious. Some small eateries then followed suit, cooking fish with pickled Chinese cabbage to serve customers. As a result, the Boiled Fish with Pickled Chinese Cabbage became popular in the early 1990s, and most restaurants offer this specialty all over the country.

酸菜鱼始于重庆江津的渔船上。据传，当地渔民会把大鱼卖掉换钱，剩下的小鱼给当地农家换取酸菜。渔夫们将酸菜和鲜鱼烩于一锅，想不到，这道食物味道还真鲜美。于是，一些小餐馆也纷纷效仿，用酸菜烹鱼招待顾客。上世纪90年代初，酸菜鱼开始流行，如今，全国大多数餐馆都有这道特色美食。

34 Emperor Qianlong and the Boiled Fish Head with Bean Curd 鱼头豆腐与乾隆皇帝

According to legend, Emperor Qianlong disguised himself to visit Wushan when touring the regions south of the Yangtze River. When he reached the hillside, a heavy rain poured down and soaked him like a wet chicken. Hungry and frustrated, he went to a house to find something to eat. The owner of the house was Wang Runxing, a snack peddler. However, the peddler had no other food except a fish head and a piece of bean curd. So he put the fish head, bean curd, and some ingredients in a casserole and began to stew them. Before long, Emperor Qianlong ate the stewed food. While eating, he found it more delicious than the royal delicacies.

据传，乾隆皇帝在游江南时，微服游玩吴山。到了半山腰，大雨倾盆而下，把他淋成了落汤鸡。乾隆帝饥肠辘辘，十分沮丧，便来到一户人家找食物充饥。这家主人叫王润兴，是经营小吃的买卖人。然而，这个买卖人除了一个鱼头和一块豆腐外，再没有别的食物。于是，他把鱼头、豆腐和一些配料放进砂锅炖起来。没过多久，乾隆帝吃上了炖菜。在吃的时候，他发现这比宫廷的美味佳肴还要可口。

Later, when Emperor Qianlong returned to the capital city, where he had chefs in the imperial kitchen cook the food he had eaten before. However, whatever the chefs did, the taste couldn't satisfy the emperor.

后来，乾隆帝回到京城，就让御膳房做他先前吃过的这道菜。然而，无论御厨怎么做，味道都不能让他满意。

Once again, Emperor Qianlong went to Wushan, where he saw Peddler Wang again in his shack. He said to Wang, "You are good at cooking. Why don't you open a restaurant?" Wang said, "I have not enough food to eat. How can I afford to open a restaurant?" So Emperor Qianlong gave him five hundred taels of silver. In addition, he also wrote down three characters "皇饭儿" (imperial eatery), as well as his name. By then, Wang realized that the visitor was the emperor, so he quickly knelt in front of the emperor to show his deep respect.

乾隆帝再次来到吴山，又在那间破屋子见到姓王的买卖人。他对王润兴说："你的烹饪手艺好，怎么不开个饭铺呢？"王润兴说："我自个儿都吃不饱，怎么开得起饭铺呢？"于是，乾隆帝赏赐他五百两银子，还写下"皇饭儿"三个大字，落款"乾隆"。这时，王润兴才知道来客是当今皇上，便立刻跪下，以表敬意。

Wang Runxing then opened an eatery. In the eatery, he put up a plaque which read, "皇饭儿." Soon after the news got around, people flocked to the eatery to eat. Meanwhile, in order to attract more customers, Wang further improved his skill in cooking. Other local restaurants followed suit, eventually making the Boiled Fish Head with Bean Curd popular in Hangzhou.

于是，王润兴开了一家小饭馆，并在店内高悬牌匾，上面写道："皇饭儿"。消息传开后，人们成群结队地到这家饭馆就餐。同时，为了吸引更多顾客，王润兴不断提高烹饪手艺。当地其他餐馆也纷纷效仿，鱼头豆腐最终誉满杭城。

35 The Legend of the Fish Ball and the First Emperor of the Qin Dynasty 鱼丸的传说与秦始皇

According to legend, the first emperor of the Qin Dynasty liked to eat fish and fish was a necessity for his every meal. However, he required his chef to remove fish bones while cooking. If he ate fish with bones in it, he would order the chef to die. Several chefs died for this.

传说，秦始皇好吃鱼，每餐必须有鱼，而且要求烹制时要去除鱼刺。如果有鱼刺，则赐厨师死，有好几名厨师为此丧命。

One day, when one chef was cooking for the emperor, he

found that he had to cook fish. He worried that he would not be able to completely remove the fish bones from the fish while cooking, so he struck the fish with the back of a kitchen knife to vent his fear. Bang, bang, bang… The result surprised him because he found that the bones of fish had been automatically exposed, and the fish had been beaten to a fish pulp.

一天，一名厨师在做御膳时，发现需要烹鱼。他担心烹鱼时无法将鱼刺完全取出，于是就用菜刀背击打鱼身，以释放自己的恐惧情绪。砰、砰、砰…… 其结果让他感到意外，鱼刺自动显露出来，鱼肉变成了鱼茸。

Just then, a call came from the palace, saying that it was time for the emperor to have dinner. The chef had an idea on the spur of the moment. He quickly picked out the fish bones and shaped the fish pulp into smooth balls. Without hesitation, he put the balls into the soup and cooked them quickly.

就在这时，宫中叫起传膳。厨师急中生智，迅速挑出鱼刺，再把鱼茸团成光滑的丸子，不假思索地将丸子投入汤中加快烹煮。

After a while, the fish balls began to float in the boiling soup. Each one was crystal white, and tasted soft and fresh. The fish balls were then presented to the emperor, who tasted the ball and was unstinting in his praise. Of course, the chef was rewarded. Later, this method of making fish balls spread from the court and was widely used among the common people.

过了一会儿，鱼丸就漂浮在沸腾的汤面上，个个色泽洁白，尝之柔软鲜嫩。鱼丸呈到皇上面前，他尝了尝，赞不绝口。当然，御厨得到了奖赏。后来，这种制作鱼丸的方法从宫廷流传出来，在民间广泛使用。

36 Two Stories About Perch
鲈鱼的两个故事

A perch dish is a tasty fish food. "The Later Ode to the Red Cliff," one of the *ci* poems by Su Dongpo of the Song Dynasty, describes the appearance of the perch: "At dusk today, I cast my fishing net and caught fish. Its large mouth and thin scales make it look like a Songjiang perch."

鲈鱼是一种美味的鱼类食物。宋代苏东坡的词作《后赤壁赋》描写了鲈鱼的外貌："今者薄暮，举网得鱼，巨口细鳞，状如松江之鲈。"

Here are two well-known stories of the perch.

有两则人们熟知的有关鲈鱼的故事。

The first story comes from *The Romance of the Three Kingdoms*. Once in winter, Cao Cao held a large banquet in Xuchang to entertain groups of his officials. During the banquet, an unexpected guest arrived. His name was Zuo Ci.

一则故事源自《三国演义》。一年冬天，曹操在许昌办宴席款待众多官员。期间，一名不速之客驾到，他就是左慈。

When Zuo Ci saw the banquet offer a fish dish, he said, "You should eat Songjiang perch when you eat fish."

左慈见席上有鱼，便道："吃鱼就得吃松江鲈鱼。"

Cao Cao replied, "How could I get Songjiang perch in this area?"

曹操道："此地怎样能弄到松江鲈鱼？"

"I have some perch in my backyard pond. I can catch some with a fishing rod," Zuo replied. After saying that, he took a fishing rod and went to the pond, where he soon caught some perch.

左慈答道："我家后院池塘养了几条鲈鱼，可用鱼竿钓到几条。"说完，他拿起鱼竿，走到池塘边，很快就钓到了鲈鱼。

"Well, well–" said Cao Cao, "Did you really get these perch from the pond, or did you bring them here with you?"

"啊！"曹操问道，"这些鲈鱼真的是从池塘里弄来的，还是你带来的？"

"Perch usually have two gills, but the Songjiang perch have four gills. If you doubt it, please come and have a look."

"鲈鱼通常有两鳃，而松江鲈鱼有四鳃。若有疑问，请来看看。"

Everyone came close up for a look. As expected, each perch he caught had four gills.

大家凑近观看。不出所料，钓到的鲈鱼皆有四鳃。

Cao Cao was so pleased that he immediately sent someone to cook the four-gill perch. When the dish was served and tasted, everyone was full of praise.

曹操大喜，速派人烹制"四腮鲈鱼"。鲈鱼上桌，大家品尝后，都赞不绝口。

The second story occurred in the Jin Dynasty. There was an official named Zhang Han who served in a government office in Luoyang. One day in autumn, Zhang saw someone selling perch in a market. It reminded him of perch and water shields in his hometown Wu Prefecture. He said, "The value of life lies in enjoyment. How could I secure an official position thousands of miles away, just for the sake of fame and official title?" So, he resigned his official post and returned to his hometown. His excuse for resignation was that he longed for his hometown dish of chopped perch and the soup of water shields. Since then, "longing for water shields and perch" has been synonymous with "homesickness."

另一则故事发生在晋朝。一名叫张翰的官员在洛阳出仕。秋日，张翰在集市上看见有人在卖鲈鱼，这使他想起了家乡吴郡的鲈鱼和莼菜。他说道："人生贵得适意尔，何能羁宦数千里以要名爵？"于是，他辞官返乡。请辞的理由是，思念家乡的鲈鱼脍和莼菜羹。此后，"莼鲈之思"成为乡愁的同义词。

37 Abalone, a Delicious Food in Ancient Times 珍肴美味鲍鱼历史悠久

The food abalone has a therapeutic effect on *yin* deficiency in a human body and is often given to relatives and friends as a lucky gift. In addition, on the New Year's Day or other festivals, abalone is seen as an auspicious food to entertain friends, relatives or important visitors at a dining table.

鲍鱼这种食物对人体具有滋阴功效，人们通常会把鲍鱼当作吉祥礼品馈赠亲朋好友。此外，在新年或其他节日，鲍鱼是款待亲朋好友和重要来客的吉利菜。

The Chinese have been eating abalone for a long time. According to *Records of the Historian* by Sima Qian, abalone was regarded as a precious and delicious food. *The Biography of Wang*

Mang in *The Book of the Earlier Han Dynasty* says, "Wang Mang's rebellion would soon be destroyed. He didn't feel like eating, but only drank wine and ate abalone livers." However, in ancient times, abalone could only be eaten by members of the aristocracy. It was listed as one of the eight delicacies during the Ming and Qing dynasties.

在中国，吃鲍鱼有着悠久的历史。《史记》称鲍鱼为"珍肴美味"。《汉书·王莽传》记载："王莽事将败，悉不下饭，唯饮酒，啖鲍鱼肝。"在古代，只有贵族才能吃到鲍鱼。明清时期，鲍鱼被列为八大美食之一。

In the Qing Dynasty, when senior officials from coastal regions had an opportunity of going to the capital for an audience with the emperor, they would prepare gifts, including dried abalone. According to the hierarchical system, a first-rank official would offer pieces of abalone, each weighing 0.5 kilogram. Those of lower ranks would correspondingly present much smaller abalone.

清朝，沿海地区的高官若有机会进京觐见皇帝，皆会准备包括干鲍鱼在内的礼物。按照等级制度，一品官员会呈上几只鲍鱼，每只重0.5公斤，职位低的官员会送上相应小得多的鲍鱼。

Toward the end of the Qing Dynasty, the Tan's Home-Style Cuisine appeared in Beijing. Its menu included two well-known dishes. One was the Braised Abalone in Soy Sauce, and the other the Abalone in Oyster Sauce.

将近清末年间，北京有了谭家菜，其菜单上有两道名菜，即红烧鲍鱼和蚝油鲍鱼。

At present, fresh, dried or canned abalone is available in China. It is usually cooked in several ways, such as deep-frying, braising, simmering, or grilling. The best taste is steamed or stewed abalone although it can also be cooked and mixed with salad dressing.

目前，在中国可以买到新鲜鲍鱼、干鲍鱼或罐装鲍鱼。通常烹调鲍鱼有几种方法，如炸、红烧、文炖、烧烤。虽然也可以拌上调料做出鲍鱼沙拉，但是味道最好的要算清蒸或文炖鲍鱼。

38 Qiaojiao Beef from Suji Town of Leshan 乐山苏稽跷脚牛肉

It is said that Qiaojiao Beef was first produced by a villager named Zhou Tianshun in the late Qing Dynasty. Zhou's exact background is unknown, but we do know that he was a butcher.

据说，跷脚牛肉是清末一位名叫周天顺的村民发明的。他的确切背景不详，只知道他是个屠夫。

At that time, the beef in Leshan of Sichuan mainly came from Zhoucun Village near Suji town. Many cattle were slaughtered in the village every day, but there was still a shortage of beef. The cattle entrails were often discarded after slaughtering.

当时，四川乐山的牛肉主要来自苏稽附近的周村。村里每天要屠宰很多牛，但牛肉仍然供不应求。牛的内脏常常在屠宰后被丢弃不用。

One day, Zhou came out after he had slaughtered cattle. By then, piles of cattle entrails were dumped by the roadside and on the banks of the river. He thought it was wasteful, so he picked up some entrails and went home with them. When he got home, he washed the entrails with water and then cooked them in a soup pot with some seasonings. After cooking, Zhou tasted the entrails in the pot and found them delicious, so he shared the cooked entrails with the locals. After eating, everyone complimented them on their good taste.

一天，周天顺宰了牛后走了出来。当时，成堆的牛杂被丢弃在路边和河岸上。他觉得可惜，便捡了些带回家。到家后，他用水把牛杂清洗干净，然后在汤锅里加了些佐料烹煮牛杂。煮熟后，周天顺尝了尝，感觉味道很好，于是便与大家分享。大家吃过后，都称赞味道不错。

"Wouldn't it be great if I could cook all the discarded entrails for more people to eat?" Zhou thought. So he built a simple stove out of clay and bamboo crates by the Suji River. On the top of the stove was a large iron pot, and beside the stove stood by a long table. The pot was filled with water and some seasonings, and Zhou threw the cleaned entrails into the pot to cook. Soon the boiling soup gave off a rich smell all around. Many vegetable sellers and load-carrying laborers came by, eating the cooked entrails. After eating, they found the food tasty and refreshing. Later, it became known locally as the Soup Pot.

周天顺心想："如果我能够把这些不要的牛杂烹煮，给更多的人吃，岂不是很棒吗？"于是，他在苏稽河边用篾篓和黏土做了个简易土灶，土灶上架起一口大铁锅，旁边摆上一张长桌，锅里加满水和一些调料。周天顺把洗净的牛杂放入锅里煮，沸腾的浓汤很快香气四溢。许多卖菜的、扛东西的路过此地，便来吃煮好的牛杂。他们吃过后，都觉得好吃而且饱腹。后来，当地人称之为"汤锅儿"。

The Soup Pot was very popular among the laborers at the bottom of society because it was very low in price. Later, it turned out that not only the entrails were tasty, but also the beef was delicious, too. As more and more people came to eat the entrails and beef in the soup pot, many diners had to stand up while eating because there were not enough benches around. As they ate, they lifted one foot, stepping on the bar under the long table. Later, people called the soup pot Qiaojiao Beef. Qiaojiao means "lifting one's leg."

由于汤锅儿价格很便宜，很受底层劳动人民的欢迎。后来发现，不仅牛杂味道好，牛肉也很好吃。随着越来越多的人来吃牛杂和牛肉汤锅儿，许多人不得不站着吃，一边吃，一边抬起一只脚，踩在长桌下的横木上，所以再后来，人们把这种汤锅儿叫作"跷脚牛肉"。

39 The Mongol Cavalry and the Beef Jerky 蒙古骑兵与牛肉干

The Beef Jerky, also known as Hand-Shredded Dried Beef or Air-Dried Beef, is a specialty of Xinjiang and Inner Mongolia. Since ancient times, local herdsmen on the grassland have had the custom of drying beef jerk, which is often used to entertain distinguished guests.

牛肉干是新疆和内蒙古特产，又称"手撕牛肉干"或"风干牛肉"。自古以来，草原牧民就有晒牛肉干的习俗。牛肉干常用于招待贵客。

The Beef Jerky was closely associated with the Mongol cavalry when Genghis Khan founded the Mongol Empire. After a cow was slaughtered, its beef was left to dry in the air. The dry beef was then ground to powder and packed into bags. The cavalrymen carried their ground beef jerky bags on their backs, and wherever they went, they could eat it with water. Therefore, the Beef Jerky, known as "Genghis Khan's army provisions for the on-march cavalrymen," played a very important role in the expedition.

成吉思汗建立蒙古帝国时，蒙古骑兵与牛肉干有着不解之缘，一头牛宰杀后，牛肉晾干，然后磨成粉末，装入口袋。蒙古骑兵将其背在身上，无论走到哪里，便可用水冲饮牛肉干粉。牛肉干在远征作战中起着很重要的作用，被誉为"成吉思汗的行军粮"。

40 Huainan Beef Soup, a Well-Known Snack in Henan and Anhui

豫皖名小吃：淮南牛肉汤

Huainan Beef Soup is a well-known snack in the regions across Henan and Anhui. This soup contains dozens of nourishing herbs and marinating materials. It is made by a traditional technique, and the process is time consuming. In addition, the soup will taste better if bean noodles are added.

淮南牛肉汤是豫皖一带名小吃。这种汤选用几十种滋补药材及卤料，按照传统工艺熬制，过程很耗时。此外，如果加入粉条，汤的味道会更好。

According to historical records, in 957, Zhao Kuangyin led his troops to attack Shouchun, a town located at present-day Shouxian County of Anhui Province. General Liu Renzhan and his men fought to defend the town. Zhao's troops were unable to conquer it though they attacked tenaciously. As days went by, without reinforcements or supplies, Zhao and his men were trapped in an awkward situation. At that time, locals became anxious. At last, they slaughtered cattle and cooked them in a pot. Then they sent the beef soup to Zhao's barracks, where his men drank the soup, and their morale was greatly inspired. With vigorous effort, they conquered Shouchun.

据史料记载，957年，赵匡胤率兵攻打寿春（今安徽寿县）。守将刘仁詹和其部下顽强守城。赵部勇猛进攻，但还是难以攻克寿春。久而久之，赵匡胤及其部下因无援军和粮草而陷入困境。当时，地方百姓焦虑不安，他们最后纷纷宰牛，放在锅里烹煮，然后把牛肉汤送入赵营。赵部官兵喝了牛肉汤后士气大振，一鼓作气攻破了寿春城。

In 959, after the Military Mutiny at Chenqiao, Zhao came to the throne and proclaimed himself emperor. However, he never forgot the Huainan Beef Soup. Accordingly, the Huainan Beef Soup was believed to be "a divine soup" or "the soup that saved the emperor from the dangerous situation."

959年，陈桥兵变，赵匡胤即位称帝，但他始终忘不了淮南牛肉汤。淮南牛肉汤由此被传为"神汤"或"救驾汤"。

During the Qianlong years of the Qing Dynasty, Zhang Zheng, a Huainan native and grand secretary, resigned from office and returned to his hometown, where he updated the recipe of the Huainan Beef Soup according to the royal secret one. Later, he passed on his recipe to his descendants and the Huainan Beef Soup with its unique flavor spread everywhere along the Huaihe River and other regions.

清乾隆年间，淮南人大学士张政告老还乡。他根据宫廷秘方改进了淮南牛肉汤的做法，后又将配方传于后人，从而风味独特的淮南牛肉汤传遍了淮河两岸和其他地区。

41 The Origin of Sliced Beef and Ox Tongue in Chili Sauce 夫妻肺片的由来

According to legend, toward the end of the Qing Dynasty, in Chengdu there were many vendors, who carried baskets either on their shoulders or in their hands along the streets and alleys. They sold the cold dish known as Sliced Beef and Ox Tongue in Chili Sauce. The main ingredients were the low-cost assorted entrails that had been cleaned and stewed. The stewed entrails were sliced and then added with soy sauce, chili oil, spicy pepper, powder of the Chinese prickly ash, sesame seeds and other seasonings. Because of its unique taste and low price, this cold dish was very popular, especially among rickshaw men, porters and poor students.

相传，清朝末年，许多小贩挑担或手提篮子，在成都街头巷尾叫卖凉拌肺片。凉拌肺片的主要食材是低廉的什锦牛杂碎，经清洗、卤煮、切片后，佐以酱油、红油、辣椒、花椒面、芝麻等调味料凉拌而成。这道凉菜风味独特，价格低廉，特别受到拉黄包车的、脚夫和穷苦读书人的喜爱。

Guo Chaohua was a native of Chengdu. In the 1930's, he worked with his wife to prepare the cold dish of Sliced Beef and Ox Tongue in Chili Sauce. Afterward, the couple walked along the streets, peddling their cold dishes from the baskets they carried. Due to the use of leftover bits and pieces from beef shops, their cold dishes were low in price, but tasty and popular among the locals. Gradually, the locals came to call their cold dishes *fuqi feipian* (Husband and Wife's Sliced Beef and Ox Tongue in Chili Sauce).

郭朝华是成都人。20世纪30年代，他和妻子一道制作凉拌肺片，夫妻俩提着篮子走街串巷，叫卖自己做的凉拌肺片。由于使用的是牛肉铺的边角料，凉拌菜价格便宜，但味道好，颇受当地人欢迎。渐渐地，人们就把他们做的凉拌菜称为“夫妻肺片”。

In 1933, Guo and his wife opened a shop near the Banbian Bridge in Chengdu. The shop was formally named as Fuqi Feipian. They changed its site several times, and it was finally moved to the Tidu West Street in the downtown area. Meanwhile, in addition to Sliced Beef and Ox Tongue in Chili Sauce, it also offered beef noodles and other varieties. Later, through the hard work of several generations, Sliced Beef and Ox Tongue in Chili Sauce has become a famous cold dish far and wide.

1933年，郭氏夫妇在成都半边桥附近开了一家门店，店名正式命名为“夫妻肺片”。后几经变迁，该店最终迁至市区提督西街。同时，除了夫妻肺片以外，店里还供应牛肉面等品种。后来，经过几代人的努力，夫妻肺片成为远近闻名的冷盘菜肴。

42 Stories About the Origin of the Instant-Boiled Mutton 涮羊肉的由来

Instant-Boiled Mutton, also known as Mutton Hot Pot, is one of the easiest dishes to serve. People can be seated around the table, and all must have chopsticks, because they will use their chopsticks to dip the raw food into the pot, and within a few minutes use their chopsticks again to retrieve strips of meat and vegetables. The hot pot is a delightful dinner indoors in winter, and outdoors during spring or summer evenings.

涮羊肉又称“羊肉火锅”，是最容易做的餐食之一。人们围坐在桌子四周，都得拿着筷子将生食蘸入锅里，几分钟内再用筷子夹出条状的肉和蔬菜食用。冬天在室内，春夏夜晚在户外，这种火锅是一种令人愉快的餐食。

Well, there are different stories on the origin of the Instant-Boiled Mutton. According to one story, Wang Shichong of the Sui Dynasty, who proclaimed himself Emperor of the State of Zheng, fought hard in Luoyang area against the army led by Li Shimin. Li dispatched almost all his soldiers and generals to surround Luoyang City, while he took only ten men with him on the snow-covered Mt. Beimang.

关于涮羊肉的起源，可谓众说纷纭。根据一则说法：隋朝的王世充称帝，建郑国，在洛阳与李世民率领的军队激战。李世民派出几乎所有的将士包围洛阳城，而他只带着十个卫兵待在白雪覆盖的北邙山。

Soon, Li was surprised to find himself surrounded by Wang's army. To make matters worse, he had no way to send an emergency message to his main force for help. Although Wang's men surrounded Li and his small group, they did not dare to move forward and capture Li. They thought that Li was so cunning that he might have set a trap for them to fall into. Wang sent Shan Xiongxin to go up to the mountain and negotiate a ceasefire with Li.

不久，李世民惊讶地发现自己被王世充的军队团团围住。更糟糕的是，他还没有法子向大部队求援。王世充的人围住了李世民和那几个士兵，但不敢向前去抓李世民。他们认为李世民诡诈，可能会设下陷阱，于是，王世充便派单雄信上山与李世民谈判休战。

Li met Shan, but he refused a ceasefire. Li said, "General, if you really want a ceasefire, can you let me think it out carefully?

I will reply to you tomorrow morning." He continued, "General, I'd like to borrow your fur overcoats so we can spend the night in the mountains; otherwise we will all freeze to death here."

李世民见了单雄信，拒绝休战。他说道："将军，若真有和解诚意，可容我三思，明早听回音。"又说："将军，可借皮大衣一用，便可在山上歇宿，否则会在此地冻死。"

Shan accepted Li's proposals. At night, a wild goat passed by the camp, where Li and his men were staying. The soldiers seized the goat for food. Li didn't think that bulky pieces of mutton could be well cooked in a short time. So he had his men cut mutton into thin slices, pierce the slices with sticks, and then soak them into boiling water. The soldiers followed Li's advice and ate the boiled mutton slices. Afterward, Li and his men put on the fur overcoats and pretended to be a patrol team of Wang's army. They walked down the mountain and managed to escape from Wang's encirclement. Later, Li named the mutton slices Instant Boiled Mutton.

单雄信应允了李世民的提议。当晚，一只野羊经过李世民和士兵们的营地，士兵们抓住山羊为食。李世民怕大块的羊肉在短时间内煮不熟，便让士兵们把羊肉切成薄片，用木棍穿上羊肉片，再浸入沸水里。士兵们听从李世民的建议，吃了煮羊肉片。然后，李世民和士兵们穿上毛皮大衣，冒充王世充的巡逻队下了山，成功逃离了包围圈。后来，李世民就把这种羊肉片命名为"涮羊肉"。

According to the second story, Kublai Khan once went south with his main army forces on an expedition. One day, exhausted by the long journey, Kublai Khan ordered his men to stop for a rest and prepare a meal. He also asked his cook to stew mutton for him.

根据另一则说法：一次，忽必烈统帅大军南下远征。一天，忽必烈因长途跋涉而疲惫不堪，便吩咐部下停下来休息，预备饭菜。此外，他还让厨师给他炖羊肉。

His cook had slaughtered some sheep, and while he was cutting them, a scout on horseback arrived and reported to Kublai Khan the arrival of the enemy.

厨师宰了几只羊，可他正在切肉之时，侦察兵策马而至，禀告敌军追赶来了。

Kublai Khan immediately ordered his troops to advance to the battlefield. At the same time, he shouted to his cook, "Mutton! Mutton! "

忽必烈一边下令部队挺进战场，一边喊着："羊肉！羊肉！"

His cook quickly sliced mutton, and then tossed the slices into boiling water and stirred them slightly. After that, he put them into a bowl, sprinkled salt over them and presented the boiled mutton slices to Kublai Khan.

厨师迅速地将羊肉切成薄片，放入沸水中，稍加搅动后就把羊肉盛到碗里，撒上盐后将熟羊肉片端给了忽必烈。

Kublai Khan ate the meat. Then he jumped onto his horse and rushed to the battlefield. When he won the battle, he held a feast to celebrate the victory. In addition, he specially ordered the sliced mutton that he had eaten before the battle.

忽必烈吃了肉，然后飞身上马，冲向战场。获胜后，忽必烈举办酒宴庆祝胜利。此外，他还特意要了此前吃的羊肉片。

This time, the cook sliced tender mutton and added some other ingredients to make it even tastier. He said to Kublai Khan, "This dish has no name yet. Please bestow a name on this dish, Your Excellency."

这次，厨师将嫩羊肉切成薄片，又加入了一些佐料，使其更加美味可口。他对忽必烈道："此菜尚无名称，请大人赐名。"

Kublai Khan replied with a smile, "Let's call it the Instant-Boiled Mutton." From then on, this dish became a delicacy in the palace.

忽必烈微笑道："就叫涮羊肉吧！"从此，涮羊肉成了宫廷一道佳肴。

43 The Discovery of Stone Reliefs of Kebabs 烤肉串画像石的发掘

Mutton Kebabs are a popular barbecue food. At present, kebabs are not limited to mutton. Beef, chicken, fish, and many vegetables can also be grilled. The main seasonings for kebabs are chili pepper and cumin. In addition, people often add some other seasonings to satisfy the tastes of young and old alike.

羊肉串是很受欢迎的烧烤食物。目前，烤肉串不仅局限于羊肉，还可以是牛肉、鸡肉、鱼肉以及许多蔬菜。辣椒和孜然是烤肉串的主要调味料，但是人们还会加入一些其他佐料，口味更加丰富，老少皆宜。

In the 1980's, archaeologists excavated a dilapidated ancient tomb in Wulipu Village of Linyi City in the south of Shandong. The tomb's history dates back to the remaining years of the Eastern Han Dynasty, and among its remains are two stone reliefs with images of barbecues. According to the research, the meat grilled by the figures in the two reliefs is beef and mutton. Most notably, on the upper right of one relief is a vivid scene of four men, one piercing pieces of meat with a skewer, one grilling meat, and the other two waiting nearby to take away the grilled meat. The barbecuer kneels in front of a charcoal stove, turning the skewers with his left hand and fanning them with his right hand. These two stone reliefs reflect the local diet customs in the southern region of Shangdong about 1,800 years ago.

20世纪80年代，考古学家在鲁南临沂市内五里堡村发掘出一座残破的古墓。墓室为东汉末年之墓，墓的遗迹中有两块烤肉串画像石。据研究，这两块画像石上画的烤肉是牛羊肉。最值得注意的是，一块画像石的右上方是一幅生动的四人场景图：一人在用扦子串肉，一人在烤肉，另外两个人在旁边等待取走烤肉串。烤肉者跪在炭槽前，左手翻动肉串，右手扇着扇子。这两块画像石反映了约1,800年前的鲁南民间饮食风俗。

In the early Ming Dynasty, when one wanted to grill beef or mutton, he/she would cut them into small cubes first, then marinate them with chopped green onions, salt, and fermented soybean sauce for a while, and finally grill them. In the late Ming and early Qing dynasties, the Mongols would boil large chunks of beef or mutton for a while before grilling them. In the twenty-fifth Daoguang year of the Qing Dynasty (1845), Poet Yang Jingting highly praised barbecues in the book named *Miscellaneous Poems in the Capital City*. It says, "In the dead of winter, meat is grilled and tasted really good; in front of the big wine vat, diners sit around together. Charbroiling is most appropriate for grilling tender meat, while on snowy days hard liquor is in high need." Well, at that time, the barbecues greatly appealed to many diners.

明朝初期，人们烤牛羊肉时，会先把牛羊肉切成方块，再用葱花、盐、豉汁腌制一下，最后再烤。明末清初，蒙古族人则是把大块的牛羊肉煮一会儿，然后再烤。清道光二十五年（1845），诗人杨静亭在《都门杂咏》中赞道："严冬烤肉味堪饕，大酒缸前围一遭。火炙最宜生嗜嫩，雪天争得醉烧刀。"那个时候，烤肉吸引了许多食客。

44 The Folk Story About the Stir-Frying Yellow Eel at a High Temperature
爆鳝卷的民间传说

Yellow eel is the main ingredient of the Stir-Frying Yellow Eel. When the eel is stir-fried at a high temperature, it will become curved and taste tender and fresh.

黄鳝是爆鳝卷的主料。旺火爆炒后，鳝鱼卷曲，味道鲜嫩。

Behind the dish is a folk story that explains why people eat eel. A long time ago, according to legend, there was a yellow snake in Yunmeng Large Pool. The snake had magical powers and could travel across the sky. It developed its power in hopes that some day it could attain the *dao* and ascend to the splendid dragon palace.

这道菜有一则民间传说，讲述了吃鳝鱼的缘由。相传很早以前，云梦大泽里有一条黄蛇，这条蛇有神奇魔力，会腾云驾雾。它不断提升功力，渴望早日得道，住进辉煌的龙宫。

Once, the snake took part in a pilgrimage-to-Guanyin (Goddess of Mercy) assemblage attended by thousands of celestial beings. He wished that he would attain the *dao* at an early stage.

一次，黄蛇去了观音朝拜会，参加者有成千上万的神仙，黄蛇希望早日修成正果。

Guanyin saw through its intention when the snake came to visit her. However, Guanyin, out of her perfect compassion and kindness, asked the snake to do more good things and accumulate more charitable and pious deeds within three years, so that it could ascend into the circle where the celestial beings resided. Guanyin also gave the snake *jindan* (a pill made by refining cinnabar), requiring the snake to turn into a human being and practice spiritual cultivation patiently.

黄蛇拜谒观音时，观音识破了其用意。然而，观音大慈大悲，吩咐黄蛇在三年内要多做好事，积善积德，这样便可升天仙界。此外，观音赐给金丹一颗，命其变换成人耐心修炼。

The yellow snake swallowed the pill and soon became a rich man who called himself Lord Huang. In the beginning, he abided by the law and behaved himself well. However, as time passed, he abandoned Guanyin's advice and gradually revealed his sly nature, colluding with local evil gentry and ruffians to bully the poor around. In order to cover up his misdeeds, his accomplices hung up a gold-letter plaque, which said "There is no greater joy than in doing charitable deeds."

黄蛇吞了金丹，很快变成了一个富翁，自称黄员外。起初，他还能遵纪守法，行为端正。然而，随着时间推移，他背弃了观音的教诲，逐渐显露出狡猾的本性，与当地劣绅勾结，危害四周的穷苦百姓。为了掩盖罪行，他的同伙给他挂上了"为善最乐"的金匾。

There was an honest scholar who couldn't bear what Lord Huang had done. He said to someone in private, "Lord Huang is aptly named if 人 is added to the left side of the character 为."

一位正直的书生，对黄员外所作所为无法忍受。他私下对人道："在'为'的左边加上'人'旁，才名副其实呢。"

Chinese characters are square characters. Most of them are composed of two parts, namely a left part and a right part, or a top part and a bottom part. When 人 appears on the left of 为, it turns into another character 伪, which means "hypocrisy." So it would be most appropriate if the plaque reads "There is no greater joy than in being hypocritical."

汉字是方块字，大多由两部分组成，左右结构，或上下结构。当"人"放在"为"的左边时，就成了"伪"字，意思是"虚伪"。所以，匾上题写"伪善最乐"是最恰当不过的了。

Upon hearing of what the scholar said, Lord Huang immediately arrested the scholar's whole family and tortured them. He even attempted to rape the scholar's daughter. At this very moment, Guanyin arrived at the spot and chanted, "To be a dragon or a celestial being is just your wishful thinking. Any human being can slaughter you to make a dish to eat." The Stir-Frying Yellow Eel was said to become popular far and wide since then.

此语传到黄员外耳中，他立即把书生全家抓起来，严刑拷打。他甚至企图强奸书生的女儿。就在这时，观音来到现场，吟道："成龙登仙你妄想，任人宰杀当菜吃。"从此"爆鳝卷"便流行起来。

45 The Shrimp Soup with Crispy Rice Crust Rated as "the Best Dish in the Country"

虾仁锅巴被评为"天下第一菜"

The Best Dish in the Country, also known as the Shrimp Soup

with Crispy Rice Crust, is a traditional specialty of Wuxi in Jiangsu Province. Here is the way to make this dish. Make chicken soup with shrimp and some other ingredients. When the soup becomes thick, pour it into a bowl, and then place the fried rice crust in a separate bowl. While the thick soup is boiling hot, pour it onto the hot rice crust, and serve.

天下第一菜又称“虾仁锅巴”，是江苏无锡的传统名菜。其制作方式如下：用虾仁等辅料熬鸡汤；熬成后，倒进碗里，然后将炸好的锅巴放在另一碗里；趁汁汤滚烫时，把汁汤浇在热锅巴上，即可上桌食用。

Legend has it that Emperor Qianlong, once dressed in plain, went to Suxi when he was touring the regions south of the Yangtze River. As night fell, he came to a small restaurant for dinner. However, there were only some leftovers in the kitchen. In spite of this, the chef shoveled the rice crust out of a rice cooker, broke it up into several pieces and placed them on a plate. Then he made chicken soup with leftovers, such as stewed shrimp meat and fried chicken shreds. When the mixture thickened, he poured the hot mixture onto the crust pieces, making a short, high-pitched sound and exuding a savory smell of rice and chicken soup. After eating, the emperor highly praised the food, saying that it tasted much better than the food of a royal feast.

据传，乾隆皇帝下江南时，一日微服私访苏溪。夜幕降临时，他来到一家小店用餐，可厨房里只有些剩饭剩菜。尽管如此，厨师还是从米饭锅里铲出锅巴，把锅巴掰成几块入盘。然后，他用剩下的烩虾仁儿和炒鸡丝等做成鸡汤，等到汤变稠时，就把滚烫的鲜汤浇在锅巴上，与此同时，食物响起吱吱之声，也散发出米饭和鸡汤的香味。乾隆皇帝吃完后，大为赞赏，说这味道远胜于宫廷御筵上的食物。

In 1933, Chen Guofu, the then-Chairman of Jiangsu Province, once invited guests to dinner. He told them in advance that each guest should bring to dinner a well-known dish from his/her hometown. As a result, at the dinner table there appeared various well-known dishes, such as the Crispy Eel and Bone-in Meat from Wuxi, the Stewed Chicken in Soy Sauce from Changshu, the Four-Gill Perch from Songjiang, etc. On this day, Chen himself brought his home-made Tomato Soup with Rice Crust. After the dinner, this dish was rated as "the best dish in the country."

1933年，时任江苏省主席陈果夫请客。他事先叮嘱来宾各自携带本乡一道名菜来赴宴。于是，餐桌上便出现了各种名菜，如无锡的脆鳝和肉骨头、常熟的酱鸡、松江的四腮鲈鱼等。而这一天，陈果夫自己带的是家人做的番茄锅巴汤。饭后，这道菜被评为"天下第一菜"。

46 "Chen Mapo" and Mapo Tofu
麻婆豆腐与"陈麻婆"

Everyone has eaten various tofu dishes, including Mapo Tofu. Although many people have tasted Mapo Tofu, few know its history.

每个人都吃过各种豆腐菜肴，也包括麻婆豆腐。许多人虽然尝过麻婆豆腐，但很少有人知其历史典故。

Mapo Tofu, also known as Chen Mapo Tofu, was created in a small inn managed by a husband and his wife in the first Tongzhi year of the Qing Dynasty (1862). At that time, the chef in the inn was a woman named Liu. Because her husband's family name was Chen, and her face was covered with some pockmarks, locals called her Mapo Chen (Pockmarked Woman Chen) behind her back.

麻婆豆腐，即“陈麻婆豆腐”，始创于清朝同治元年（1862）一家夫妻小饭铺。当时，饭铺由刘氏掌灶，因为她夫家姓陈，脸上又有些麻子，当地人背后都叫她“陈麻婆”。

The husband-and-wife inn was located near the Wanfu Bridge outside the Northern Gate of Chengdu. The bridge was in a place where businessmen kept coming and going in every direction. One day, an oil peddler came and took a rest near the Wanfu Bridge. He bought two pieces of tofu and a little beef. Then he ladled out a spoonful of vegetable oil out of his oil basket and asked Mapo Chen to cook it for him.

夫妻店位于成都北门万福桥边，万福桥这个地方南来北往的客商不断。有一天，来了一位“油脚子”，在万福桥边歇脚。他买来两块豆腐和一点牛肉，然后从油篓子里舀上一勺菜油，请求陈麻婆代为加工。

Mapo Chen immediately accepted it. Then she began to braise tofu with the minced beef. She also added other ingredients, such as fermented soybean paste sauce and dry chili pepper. When the tofu was well done, Mapo Chen sprinkled some seed powder of Chinese prickly ash on the top of the food. Until then, the tofu in the minced beef stew was still soft and well shaped. It was excellent in color, smelt nice and tasted very good.

陈麻婆立即应允。然后，她用牛肉末烧豆腐，还加入了豆瓣酱、干辣椒等其他佐料。豆腐烧好后，陈麻婆在上面撒上些花椒粉。此时，烩在牛肉末里的豆腐绵软不烂，色香味俱全。

The tofu cooked by Mapo Chen was really excellent, and the oil peddler liked it very much. Soon, it spread around from person to person. Gradually, the inn's business prospered. Not only oil peddlers, but also some scholars and rich businessmen came here to taste the tofu cooked by Mapo Chen.

陈麻婆做的豆腐很好吃，那位贩油脚夫很是喜欢。很快，一传十，十传百，小店生意渐渐兴旺起来了。不仅有贩油脚夫，还有一些文人雅士、富商巨贾，都来这里品尝陈麻婆烧制的豆腐。

Mapo Chen had a unique skill in cooking tofu, which was quite popular with the locals. So for convenience, the inn was named Mapo Chen Tofu Shop, and the braised tofu was called Mapo Tofu. As time went by, the tofu became a Sichuan specialty with unique flavors.

陈氏对烹制豆腐有独特的烹饪技巧，深得当地人喜爱。所以为了方便，人们把小店命名为“陈麻婆豆腐店”，小店烧的豆腐称为“麻婆豆腐”。久而久之，麻婆豆腐成为四川一道风味独特的名菜。

The book named *The Overall View of Chengdu* was printed in the Guangxu years of the Qing Dynasty. According to the record in this book, the Mapo's inn and its tofu dish were already very famous at that time. Until the 1920's, the inn was as plain as ever, with old-fashioned square tables and high-legged stools. It still maintained its traditional Mapo-Tofu cooking style.

《成都通览》一书印于清朝光绪年间。根据书中记载，麻婆豆腐店和麻婆豆腐在当时就已经非常有名了。直到20世纪20年代，小店还是像以前一样简朴，有老式的方桌和高脚凳，依然保持着传统的麻婆豆腐烹饪法。

During the War of Resistance Against Japanese Aggression, many people moved to Chengdu. As the population grew, restaurants of northern and southern flavors sprang up in Chengdu. Since 1935, in order to attract more customers, the inn began to provide a wider variety of dishes. Despite of these changes, the main course was still Mapo Tofu. After the war, the people who fled to Chengdu returned home with the recipe of Chen Mapo Tofu. Gradually, this dish spread throughout the country.

抗日战争期间，许多人移居成都。随着人口增长，南北风味餐馆在成都出现。从1935年起，小店开始提供各种菜肴，以便吸引更多顾客。尽管小店发生了变化，主菜仍然是麻婆豆腐。抗日战争结束后，逃到成都的外地人回到了家乡，他们把陈氏麻婆豆腐的做法也传到全国各地。

In the early 1940's, the old inn displayed a new signboard "Chen Mapo Tofu." Meanwhile, the facilities of the inn had been modernized to provide a full range of meals. After 1949, Chen Mapo Tofu Restaurant was moved into downtown Chengdu. In 1990, Chen Mapo Sichuan Food Restaurant won the national Golden Tripod Prize; in 1992, the restaurant won the title of the "Famous Trademark" approved by Sichuan Provincial Industrial and Commercial Bureau; in 1993, "China's Time-Honored Brand" was awarded to the restaurant; and in 2002, Chen Mapo Tofu was honored with "Famous Dish of China."

上世纪40年代初，老店挂起了新招牌“陈麻婆豆腐”；同时，老店更新了设施，提供全套餐饮服务。1949年后，陈氏麻婆豆腐店搬到了成都市区。1990年，陈麻婆豆腐川菜馆荣获国家级“金鼎奖”，1992年被四川省工商局授予“著名商标”，1993年被授予“中华老字号”品牌，2002年被授予“中国名菜”称号。

47 A Palace Dish: the Bean Curd with Eight Delicious Ingredients 宫廷菜肴：八宝豆腐

The Bean Curd with Eight Delicious Ingredients was originally one of the imperial dishes during the Kangxi years of the Qing Dynasty. Emperor Kangxi liked high-quality dishes, so imperial chefs would satisfy his taste with boneless chicken, duck, fish, and pork.

八宝豆腐最初是清朝康熙年间的一道宫廷菜肴。康熙皇帝喜欢精美的菜肴，所以御厨们会用去骨鸡、鸭、鱼以及猪肉来满足皇帝的口味。

One day, the chefs cooked tender bean curd with soybeans. They added chicken soup and other minced ingredients until the soup became thick. The ingredients included pork, chicken, shrimp, ham, as well as fragrant mushrooms, mushrooms, melon seeds and pine nuts. Emperor Kangxi ate the bean curd soup, and he found the soup tasty and rich in nutrients. Therefore, the emperor named the soup the Bean Curd with Eight Delicious Ingredients because it contained eight nutrients. The emperor also had a royal scholar write down its recipe and cooking method.

一次，厨师们用大豆做了嫩豆腐，他们在嫩豆腐中加入了鸡汤和其他配料烹制，直到汤羹变稠。所加的配料有猪肉、鸡肉、虾、火腿，还有香菇、蘑菇、瓜子和松仁。康熙皇帝喝了豆腐羹，发现豆腐羹美味可口，营养丰富。因此，他将这道汤羹赐名为“八宝豆腐”，并让宫中文人把烹饪方法写成御方。

The emperor sometimes granted the recipe to his favorite officials. According to ancient documents, Emperor Kangxi arrived in Hangzhou during his southern tour. Song Muzhong, governor of Jiangsu, hosted Emperor Kangxi in Hangzhou. In return, the emperor kindly granted him the recipe of the Bean Curd with Eight Delicious Ingredients. Song Muzhong was overjoyed at this unexpected favor and regarded it as his most valuable treasure.

皇帝有时会把这个食谱赏赐给宠臣。据古文献记载，康熙皇帝下江南抵达杭州时，江苏巡抚宋牧仲接驾，作为回报，皇帝赏赐他八宝豆腐食谱。意外恩赐让宋牧仲大喜过望，倍加珍视。

Later, Emperor Kangxi gave the same recipe to another official named Xu Qianxue. Xu Qianxue then passed it on to his disciple Lou Cun, who in turn passed it on to his descendants. Finally, Wang Mengting received the recipe. During the Qianlong years of the Qing Dynasty, this bean curd soup was also known as Wangtaishou Bean Curd with Eight Delicious Ingredients because Wang's official position was "*taishou*" (prefecture chief).

后来，康熙帝又将此食谱赐给另一位叫徐乾学的官员。徐乾学不久又将它传给门生楼村，而楼村又传给他的后人。最后，王孟亭得到此谱。在乾隆年间，八宝豆腐因王孟亭任太守之职，称为“王太守八宝豆腐”。

One day, Yuan Mei, a famous gastronomist, came to visit Prefecture Chief Wang at his home, where he tasted the Bean Curd with Eight Delicious Ingredients. Later, he wrote about this recipe in his book called *Menus of the Sui Garden*. Since then, this recipe gradually spread among the locals and became a well-known dish in Hangzhou.

一天，著名美食家袁枚来到王太守家做客，品尝了八宝豆腐。后来，他将其收录于《随园食单》。自那时起，这道菜逐渐在当地流传开了，成为杭州的一道名菜。

48 Su Dongpo and the Dongpo-Styled Stewed Knuckle 东坡肘子与苏东坡

Dongpo-Styled Stewed Knuckle, named after Su Dongpo, is made with the lower part of a pig's leg. Although it has much fat, it tastes good. Many people who visit Sichuan or eat in Sichuan restaurants like to order this dish. However, why is the dish named after Su Dongpo of the Song Dynasty?

东坡肘子是以苏东坡命名的，是用猪肘做的菜肴。这道菜虽然肥肉多，但味道很好。凡是来四川的游客或在川菜馆用餐的人，大都喜欢点这道菜。那么，这道菜为什么要以宋代的苏东坡命名呢？

Su Dongpo was a remarkably accomplished writer in ancient China. In addition to his literary achievements, he also created several dishes in his lifetime. Among these dishes, the Dongpo-Styled Stewed Knuckle is well known across the country. He even brewed wine, made snacks and revised the folk menu. He wrote some culinary essays, including *An Ode to Vegetables and Roots*, *The Song of Pork*, and *The Song of Dongpo Soup*.

苏东坡是中国古代一位杰出的文学家。在他的一生中，除了在文学上的成就以外，他还创制出几道菜肴，其中，东坡肘子全国闻名。苏东坡甚至还酿酒，做小吃，创新民间菜谱，他著有烹饪随笔，如《菜根赋》《猪肉颂》和《东坡羹颂》。

Here are some interesting stories about the origin of this dish.

以下是东坡肘子的起源趣事。

Story One 传说一

According to the first story, once Su Dongpo went to Yongxiu in Jiangxi, where he cured a local peasant's child. The child's father prepared a meal to thank him. Su accepted the offer. While waiting for the meal, he looked around in the countryside. He couldn't help reciting a poetic line that read "禾草珍珠透心香" (*hecao zhenzhu touxin xiang*, the pearl-like dewdrops on the rice straws smell aromatic to my heart's content). The peasant, who was cooking pork in the kitchen, heard of Su's chanting. He thought that Su was teaching him how to prepare this dish, because his chanting sounded like "和草整煮透心香" (*he cao zheng zhu touxin xiang*, it smells aromatic to my heart's content when you cook the pork with the rice straws). Then, the peasant put the pork into the pot to cook it. The rice straws that tied the pork were also cooked in the same pot. Unexpectedly, the cooked pork brought out a pleasant taste! Chinese characters "禾" (*he*) and "和" (*he*) have the same sound although they have completely different meanings. "禾"means "rice" and "和" refers to "together with." Coincidentally, "珍珠" (*zhenzhu*, the pearl-like dewdrops) and "整煮" (*zheng zhu*, cooking the whole piece of something) have a similar sound in Chinese although they have their own tones. Therefore, it is not surprising that the peasant misunderstood what Su said upon hearing of his chanting.

一次，苏东坡去了江西永修，并为当地一个农夫的孩子医好了病。孩子的父亲备酒席以表达对他的感激之情，苏东坡接受了他的好意。在等候餐食之时，苏东坡环顾乡间，不禁吟出一句诗：“禾草珍珠透心香。”正在厨房炖肉的农夫听到了苏东坡的吟诵，以为是苏东坡在教他怎样做这道菜，因为这句诗听起来像是“和草整煮透心香”。于是，他将肉放进锅里去煮，同锅煮的还有捆肉用的稻草。出人意料的是，肉煮熟后味很香！汉字“禾”与“和”虽然意思迥异，但读音相同：“禾”意思是“大米”，“和”意思是“连同”。无独有偶，尽管“珍珠”和“整煮”的声调不同，但读音相似。因此，农夫听了苏东坡吟诵的诗句后误解了他的诗意，也就不足为奇了。

Story Two 传说二

According to the second story, this dish was actually created by Su's wife rather than Su himself. One day, his wife stewed a knuckle. Due to her negligence, she forgot to add more water to the pot, so the stewed pork skin became brown and stuck to the pot. She had no choice, but to quickly add various seasonings and stew the knuckle again, hoping that her second cooking would remove the burnt smell. Unexpectedly, the lightly brown pork was tasty when Su ate it. After that, he refined the recipe of this dish and recommended it to his friends and neighbors.

东坡肘子实际上是苏东坡的妻子做的一道菜，而不是苏东坡本人。一天，他的妻子在炖肘子，因一时疏忽，忘了给锅里多加些水，炖的猪皮变成了棕黄色，还粘在锅上。她别无选择，连忙加入各种调味料，又开始炖，期望再次烹煮可以去掉焦味。不料，苏东坡品尝后发现微微棕黄的肘子却可口好吃。此后，他改进了烹饪方法，并将这道菜推荐给他的朋友和邻居。

Story Three 传说三

According to the third story, in 1940's, there were four college students who studied at the Chinese Language Department of Sichuan University. In Chengdu, the four students opened a restaurant called "味之腴" (*weizhiyu*, flavored tastes). The signboard hung above the main entrance of the restaurant. The students insisted that they had obtained Su Dongpo's original calligraphy, which had been handed down from generation to generation. In addition, this restaurant also served the Dongpo-Styled Stewed Knuckle. They actively advertised this dish, claiming that it was cooked according to Su's secret recipe. Their efforts greatly contributed to the popularity of this dish in the country.

20世纪40年代，四川大学中文系的四名学生在成都开办了一家餐厅，取名"味之腴"。其招牌就挂在餐厅正门上方，学生们称他们得到了祖辈传下来的苏东坡书法真迹。此外，这家餐厅还供应东坡肘子。他们反复宣传这道菜，声称这是按照苏东坡秘方烹制的，从而大大促进了这道菜在全国各地的传播。

49 Su Dongpo and the Dongpo Meat 东坡肉与苏东坡

Su Dongpo was a famous writer in the history of our country. He served twice as an official in Hangzhou. During his second term when he served as the prefecture governor of Hangzhou, Su mobilized tens of thousands of locals to remove rotten soil and built a long embankment with soil on the West Lake. His project aimed to dredge the lake and help peasants use the lake to irrigate their fields. Later, the project was called Sugong Embankment.

苏东坡是我国历史上著名的文学家，曾两次到杭州任职。第二次来杭州时，他担任知州一职。期间，为了疏通湖水，帮助农民用湖水灌溉农田，苏东坡发动数万人疏浚西湖，修筑长堤。后来，长堤被称为“苏公堤”。

One day during the Spring Festival, many locals arrived at Su Dongpo's house, where they wished him a Happy New Year. At the same time, they presented pork and wine to thank him for leading locals in rebuilding the lake. After accepting the gifts, Su had his family members cut the pork into small pieces, each in a cubed shape; then he used his own method to braise them in soy sauce. When the braised pork was ready, he had his men deliver it out to the families of the laborers who were involved in the renovation of the West Lake.

春节某日，当地许多人来到苏东坡家拜年，送上猪肉和酒水，以感谢他带领大家治理湖水。苏东坡收了礼物，就叫家人把猪肉切成方形小块，然后他用自家的烹饪方法红烧猪肉。红烧肉做好后，苏东坡差人把肉送到参与整治西湖的农民家里。

At that time, there was a large restaurant nearby, and the owner saw everybody praise the pork braised by Su Dongpo. He had his chefs cut and braise pork in the same way so that he could sell it as the Dongpo Meat in his restaurant. Soon after this new dish was brought out, the restaurant's business grew rapidly. Later, other restaurants followed suit, and thus this dish became famous far and wide. Today, the Dongpo Meat is still popular in Sichuan restaurants all over the country.

当时，附近有一家大餐馆，掌柜看见大家皆称赞苏东坡的红烧猪肉，就让厨师用同样方法烹调菜肴，这样他就可以在自家餐馆以

“东坡肉”的菜名出售。这道新菜推出不久，餐馆的生意日益兴隆。其他餐馆随后纷纷效仿，这道菜便流传开来。如今，东坡肉在全国各地的川菜馆里仍然深受人们喜爱。

50 How the Fish-Flavored Shredded Pork Takes Its Name 鱼香肉丝菜名的由来

The Fish-Flavored Shredded Pork is a home-style dish in Sichuan. *Yuxiang wei* (Fish-Flavored Sauce) has become an accepted taste and the seasonings are usually a mixture of the Pixian Thick Soybean Sauce, chili garlic sauce, dry chili pepper, spring onions, onions, ginger, garlic, sugar, salt, soy sauce, and other ingredients. The delicately balanced flavors of the blended sauce tend to be salty, sweet, sour, spicy, and aromatic. When this sauce is used to stir-fry shredded pork, a fishy flavor will come out.

鱼香肉丝是四川的一道家常菜肴。鱼香味已经成了人们可以接受的味型，调味料通常由四川郫县豆瓣酱、蒜蓉辣酱、干红辣椒、葱、洋葱、姜、大蒜、糖、盐、酱油等混合而成，调配的酱汁具有咸、甜、酸、辣、香的特点。用这种酱料炒肉丝，会散发出鱼香味。

A long time ago, according to legend, there was a merchant family in Sichuan. The whole family liked eating fish. When cooking fish, they would add some spring onions, ginger, garlic, wine, vinegar and soy sauce to remove the unpleasant smell of fish and enhance the flavor. One night when the hostess was stir-frying a dish, she added all the seasonings, which were the leftovers from her fish cooking. She wasn't sure if this dish would taste good. A moment later, her husband came home from work. He went straight to the table, where he picked up the food from the dish with chopsticks. He tasted it and found the food surprisingly delicious. Happily, the husband asked his wife how it was cooked. She told him about her recipe, emphasizing the sauce she used came from the leftover seasonings of her fish cooking. Later, the family named the sauce Fish-Flavored Sauce because it tasted so good.

相传很久以前，四川有一户生意人家，全家人都喜欢吃鱼。他们烹鱼时，会加一些除腥增味的葱、姜、蒜、酒、醋和酱油等调味料。一天晚上，这家的女主人正在炒菜，她把烹鱼剩下的佐料都加了进去，也不确定这道菜是否好吃。过了一会儿，夫君做生意回到家。他径直走到餐桌前，用筷子夹起盘中的食物。他尝了尝，发现非常好吃，高兴地问妻子这道菜是怎么做的。妻子告诉他配制方法，详细叙述了是用烹鱼剩下的调味料做的酱汁。因为这种酱汁味道好，这家人后来将它取名为“鱼香味”。

The Overall View of Chengdu which was published in 1909 includes 1,328 recipes from Sichuan cuisine, with no fish-flavored dishes. This suggests that a fish-flavored dish didn't appear until after 1909. At present, Sichuan menus contain a list of fish-flavored dishes, including Fish-Flavored Eggplant, Fish-Flavored Pork Liver, Fish-Flavored Pork Kidney, and Fish-Flavored Shredded Pork.

1909年出版的《成都通览》记载了川菜食谱1,328种，但却无鱼香味菜肴，这说明鱼香味菜肴是直到1909年以后才出现的。目前，川菜食谱上有系列鱼香味菜肴，即鱼香茄子、鱼香猪肝、鱼香腰子和鱼香肉丝。

51 Braised Intestines in Brown Sauce and Jiuzhuan Intestines 红烧大肠与九转大肠

Precisely, Braised Intestines in Brown Sauce are Jiuzhuan Intestines. Its cooking method is unique. When cooking, the intestines are first boiled, then oil-fried and finally braised in a pot over a low heat. During this period, the intestines are repeatedly taken out and placed into the pot several times. The seasonings of this dish are fructus amomi, cinnamon and cardamom; other ingredients include green onions, ginger, garlic, cooking wine, clear soup, sesame oil, etc. When the intestines are well braised, sprinkle some coriander over them and then placed them onto a plate. By then, the braised intestines take on a reddish and shiny appearance, and taste good despite the fat content.

红烧大肠就是九转大肠，其做法很独特。烹饪时，先将大肠沸煮，再油爆，最后煨火焖烧，期间还出勺入锅反复数次。所用的调料有砂仁、肉桂、豆蔻，另外还有大葱、大姜、大蒜、料酒、清汤、香油等。大肠烧成后，撒上香菜，盛入盘中。此时的大肠红润透亮，肥而不腻。

In the Qing Dynasty, a businessman surnamed Du opened nine shops and restaurants in Jinan of Shandong. This businessman liked the Chinese character “九” (*jiu*, nine) very much, so the names of all his shops and restaurants started with the character “九.” Later, Du opened another restaurant in Jinan. It was called Jiuhua Mansion, and the word “九” was also used as the first character of its name.

清朝时，一位姓杜的生意人在山东济南设有九家店铺和餐馆。这位生意人特别喜欢“九”字，因此他的店铺和餐馆名号首字皆以

“九”字冠之。后来，杜老板在济南又开了一家餐馆，取名“九华楼”，名号首字也是用的“九”字。

Although the name of Jiuhua Mansion was not very famous, the food cooked by the chefs was very tasty. The most famous dishes were those cooked with a variety of entrails as the main ingredients. Braised Intestines in Brown Sauce were the specialty of Jiuhua Mansion in those days. Every time when guests came to Jiuhua Mansion, they would order this dish.

虽然九华楼招牌不那么出名，但厨师们做的菜肴却味美可口。最出名的，是那些用各种猪下水为主要食材烹调的菜肴。红烧大肠就是当时九华楼的特色菜，而每次来这里的客人都会点红烧大肠这道菜。

One day, Du invited local distinguished guests to Jiuhua Mansion for dinner, and one of the dishes served was Braised Intestines in Brown Sauce. Among the guests, a scholar tasted the intestines. He immediately praised this dish, saying that he was to give this dish a resonant name. Du replied, “Yes, please.” So the scholar said, “The dish tastes like an elixir refined by ancient alchemists. In general, the tasty elixir is referred to as the Jiuzhuan Elixir. Since you like the character ‘九,’ why not rename this dish Jiuzhuan Intestines?”

一天，杜老板宴请当地贵客来九华楼吃饭，其中一道菜是红烧大肠。贵客中有一位文人，他尝了尝这道菜，立刻赞不绝口，说要给它取个响亮的名字。杜老板答道：“好的，谢谢。”于是，他说：“这道菜吃起来犹如吃到古代炼丹术士所炼制的仙丹，而通常这种美味仙丹叫‘九转仙丹’。杜老板喜欢‘九’字，何不将这道菜改名为

‘九转大肠’呢？”

Upon hearing this, everyone applauded and highly praised the new name. Since then, the name of Jiuzhuan Intestines has been passed down from generation to generation.

众人一听，齐声叫好，皆对这个新名字赞不绝口。从那时起，“九转大肠”的美名就代代传了下来。

52 Stories of the Diced Pork in Pot 坛子肉的故事

Origin One 由来一

The Diced Pork in Pot is a traditional local snack in Jinan, Shandong Province. It is said that it was originally cooked by the Fengjilou Restaurant in Jinan during the Qing Dynasty. The restaurant's chefs made this dish by simmering rib meat, seasonings, and fragrant rice in small black enamel jars over a small fire of charcoal. In the late Qing Dynasty, many restaurants in Jinan sold this kind of pork food. However, among these restaurants, the Tongyuan Restaurant was the most famous one, for its Diced Pork in Pot had its good flavor and delicious taste.

坛子肉是山东济南的一种传统小吃。据传，这道菜始于清代，最初由济南凤集楼饭店烹制。这家餐厅的厨师把猪肋条肉、调味料、香米放进黑瓷釉的小坛子里，用木炭微火煨炖而成。清末，济南的许多餐馆经营这种肉食品。然而，在这些餐馆中，同元楼最有名气，其坛子肉味美可口，肉质浓香。

Origin Two 由来二

The Diced Pork in Pot in Sichuan has a strong local flavor. According to legend, this dish originated in rural Sichuan. During the rice-transplanting or harvest seasons, peasants were busy in the fields. If they wanted to eat meat, they had to take time to cook it, but they were afraid that by doing so it would delay their farm work. So before they went to the fields, they hastily put large pieces of pork into the jar with salt, water, and seasonings like green onion and ginger. Then they sealed the jar and simmered it. When the peasants returned home from their work, they opened the jar, and a delicious smell came out of it. Such a cooking method had also been introduced to local restaurants around.

四川的坛子肉富有地方乡土风味。据传，这道菜起源于四川农村。在插秧收割季节，农民们都在地间忙碌。如果他们想吃肉，就得花时间烹制，但这样做就会耽误农活。于是，他们在下地之前，匆忙地将大块猪肉放入坛子内，再加上盐、水、葱、姜等调味料，然后密封坛口，用小火炖制。收工回家后，启开坛口，香味就从里面散发出来。这种烹饪法也流传到当地餐馆。

Origin Three 由来三

The Diced Pork in Pot is said to have originated in Guiyang of Hunan. During the Three Kingdoms Period, Zhao Zilong led an army to quell the disturbances in Guiyang Prefecture. Due to the years of wars in Guiyang, local peasants lived in poverty, and Zhao reduced land rent and exempted them from paying taxes. Meanwhile, he called on peasants to raise pigs and work in the fields. Many peasants were roused to action by the appeal. They started to raise pigs, and created new methods, such as marinating, frying, or stewing to preserve the pork. Prior to the Ming Dynasty, pork had been marinated with Sichuan powder of Chinese prickly ash, as well as diced ginger and garlic. After the Ming Dynasty, hot chili pepper was introduced into southern Hunan, where pork has been marinated in chili pepper ever since then. In the Zhengde years of the Ming Dynasty, Guiyang's Diced Pork in Pot was introduced into the court and became a dish on the royal menu.

据说坛子肉源于湖南桂阳。三国时期，赵子龙率军平定桂阳郡。由于桂阳连年战乱，当地农民生活贫苦，赵子龙便减租免赋。与此同时，他呼吁农民养猪种田。许多农民响应号召行动起来，开始养猪，并发明了保藏猪肉的一些加工方法，如腌、炸、炖等。明朝之前，腌制猪肉用的是巴蜀花椒面、姜丁和蒜丁。明朝以后，辣椒传入湘南地区，那里的猪肉都采用辣椒腌制。明朝正德年间，桂阳坛子肉传入宫廷，成为宫廷菜肴之一。

53 The Origin of the Steamed Pork Wrapped in Lotus Leaves Related to Guan Yu and Zhou Cang
荷叶蒸肉与关羽和周仓

The Steamed Pork Wrapped in Lotus Leaves is a famous home-style dish. Although the steamed streaky pork is little fatty, it tastes fresh, soft, and not greasy. By adding some seasonings, it can be tasty even when eaten in summer.

荷叶蒸肉是一道有名的家常菜。虽然蒸出的五花肉有点肥，但吃起来鲜嫩、软糯、不腻。加上一些调味料，即使在夏天食用也感觉很可口。

It is said that the origin of the Steamed Pork Wrapped in Lotus Leaves is related to Guan Yu and Zhou Cang in the Three Kingdoms Period. Guan Yu rescued Zhou Cang, who later faithfully followed him. Legend has it that Zhou Cang's hands and feet were covered with thick hair, known as "flying hair." The flying hair was like a gust of wind blowing beneath his feet, enabling him to keep up with Guan Yu's Red-Rabbit Horse. And Zhou Cang was never afraid of the heat. As soon as a meal was ready, he grabbed the food in his hands and ate it at once. However, as time went on, Guan Yu became suspicious of Zhou Cang and feared that Zhou Cang would no longer be loyal to him.

据说，荷叶蒸肉的起源与三国时期的关羽和周仓有关。关羽救了周仓，周仓忠心耿耿地追随关羽。传说周仓手脚上长满了浓密的茸毛，称为“飞毛”。这层飞毛让他脚下生风，使他能够撵上关羽的赤兔马。周仓从不怕烫，饭菜一熟，抓起来就吃。可时间一长，关羽对周仓心存怀疑，怕他不再忠于自己了。

One night, Guan Yu deliberately slept with Zhou Cang in the same bed. The next day Guan Yu said to Zhou Cang, “The hair on your hands and feet pricked me so much that I couldn’t sleep at night.” Being loyal to Guan Yu, Zhou Cang scraped the hair off his hands and feet with his knife. From then on, Zhou Cang could not pick up hot food with his hands, nor could he catch up with Guan Yu’s horse.

一天晚上，关羽刻意与周仓同床而睡。第二天，关羽对周仓说：“你手脚上的毛扎得我一夜不能入睡。”周仓便用刀刮掉了手脚上的毛发。从此，他再也不能用手抓热食了，也追不上关羽的赤兔马了。

Once, Zhou Cang followed Guan Yu to a battlefield. On the way, chefs brought food to Guan Yu, Zhou Cang, and other men. Faced with the steaming hot food, Zhou Cang did not dare to lay his hands on it. At this time, Guan Yu asked him to wrap the food in lotus leaves. Zhou Cang did it. Unexpectedly, the cooked meat and rice wrapped in lotus leaves soon gave off a unique flavor. Later, based on this story, the Steamed Pork Wrapped in Lotus Leaves was made and it brought joy to all diners. The recipe of this dish is still popular today.

一次，周仓随关羽出征。途中，厨师给关羽、周仓等人送来饭菜。周仓面对热气腾腾的食物，却不敢下手。这时，关羽叫他把饭菜用荷叶包起来，周仓便照此做了。没想到，包在荷叶里的熟肉和米饭很快就散发出独特的香味。后来，根据这一说法，人们制作了"荷叶蒸肉"，这道菜给所有的食客带来了欢乐。至今，这样的做法仍然很流行。

54 The Legend of the Large Meatballs
狮子头的传说

Shizi tou, or the Lion's Head, is called in Yangzhou dialect *da zhanrou* (big cut meat). Legend has it that Emperor Yang Di of the Sui Dynasty took a dragon boat down the Grand Canal with his concubines and attendants. In Yangzhou, the emperor visited several places, such as Wansong Hill, Jinqian Mound, Xiangya Forest and Kuihua Mound. He was so happy that he wanted to commemorate his trip to Yangzhou. So back at his temporary residence, he summoned imperial chefs and asked them to make four dishes according to the four local scenic spots. A chef named Zhan Wang prepared the four dishes: *songshu guiyu* (Deep-Fried Sweet and Sour Mandarin Fish), *jinqian xiabing* (Deep-Fried Shrimp Cake), *xiangya jitiao* (Ivory-Shaped Chicken), and *kuihua zhanrou* (Sunflower-Shaped Meat-balls). Emperor Yang Di felt very happy after he tasted them. For a time, these four dishes became delicacies with their recipes circulating south of the Yangtze River. In addition, these four dishes were also considered to be delicious food at banquets hosted by officials and dignitaries.

狮子头，扬州当地话叫"大斩肉"。相传隋炀帝带着嫔妃随从乘坐龙舟沿大运河顺流而下。在扬州，隋炀帝游览了万松山、金钱墩、象牙林、葵花岗等地方后，龙颜大悦，想纪念此次扬州之行。于是，他回到行宫后召集御厨，让他们以当地的四处景点为题做四道菜。一位叫詹王的御厨做出了四道菜：松鼠桂鱼、金钱虾饼、象牙鸡条、葵花斩肉。隋炀帝品尝后非常高兴。一时间，这四道菜成了美味佳肴，传遍江南。此外，这四道菜也成了官员显贵宴请宾客的珍品。

In the Tang Dynasty, a man entitled Duke of the State of Xun once entertained his guests with a wide variety of delicious food. He also ordered Wei Juyuan, a famous chef in his mansion, to cook the four famous dishes: Deep-Fried Sweet and Sour Mandarin Fish, Deep-Fried Shrimp Cake, Ivory-Shaped Chicken and Sunflower-Shaped Meatballs. When the Sunflower-Shaped Meatballs were served, the guests found each giant meatball in the shape of a male lion's head. Knowing that the duke served in the army all his life, the guests said to him, "Your Excellency should wear a supreme-commander's seal, which is shaped like a nine-head lion." The duke drank down the wine and said, "Yes, 'the Lion's head' sounds better than the Sunflower-Shaped Meatballs. Why not change the name of this dish in honor of tonight's feast?" Since then, the Huaiyang menu has one more dish known as the Lion's Head (Braised or Steamed Large Meatballs).

唐代，郇国公一次宴请宾客，餐桌上有各种各样的美味。他还命府中名厨韦巨元做了四道名菜：松鼠桂鱼、金钱虾饼、象牙鸡条、葵花斩肉。当葵花斩肉端到桌上时，宾客们看见一个个巨大的肉丸形如雄狮之头。他们知道郇国公戎马半生，便说道："公应佩戴九头狮子帅印。"郇国公饮完酒后，说："对，'狮子头'比'葵花肉'壮哉，何不改之，以纪念今夕之会。"自此，淮扬名菜又添了一道红烧或清蒸狮子头。

When Emperor Qianlong of the Qing Dynasty traveled south of the Yangtze River, he brought this delicacy to the capital city, where it was added to the royal menu. In the Jiaqing years, Lin Lanchi, a native of Ganquan, composed *An Ode* of *Three Hundred Poems to the Hanjiang River*, eulogizing the Sunflower-Shaped Meatballs. It says in the foreword, "The meat is minced, or coarsely chopped into the shape of balls, which are then fried in pork or vegetable oil until the balls turn sunflower yellow. Its local name is the Sunflower-Shaped Mcatballs." His poem says, "The respected chef constantly minces the meat, until it is shaped like sunflowers and placed fresh in hands. Similarly, when diners are filled to satiety, the meat should remind them of sunflowers; meanwhile, one after another, they come to eat the meat, and who are those diners?"

清代，乾隆皇帝下江南，把这一佳肴带回京城，使之成为宫廷菜之一。嘉庆年间，甘泉人林兰痴著有《邗江三百吟》，歌咏了"葵花肉丸"。其序曰："肉以细切粗斩为丸，用荤素油煎成葵黄色，俗名葵花肉丸。"其诗云："宾厨缕切已频频，团此葵花放手新。饱腹也应思向日，纷纷肉食尔何人。"

55 Four-Happiness Meatballs
四喜丸子

It is said that there was a young man whose name was Zhang Jiuling in the Tang Dynasty. Once, he took part in the imperial examination presided over by the emperor. Fortunately, the emperor liked him so much that he intended to choose Zhang as his son-in-law. At the same time, Zhang's hometown was unfortunately destroyed by the flood, and there was no news from his parents. Zhang searched for his parents several times, but he couldn't find them until the day of his wedding. Immediately, Zhang sent for his parents and brought them back to the capital city. Right now, Zhang became the emperor's son-in-law from a poor scholar, and he met his parents again at the same time. Certainly, two happy events happened one after the other!

据说，唐朝时有个叫张九龄的年轻人。一次，他参加殿试，幸运的是，皇帝对他非常满意，有意招为驸马。就在此时，张九龄的家乡不幸遭遇水害，父母音信杳无。张九龄几经寻找，直到成婚那一天，才得知父母的下落，便立刻派人把他们接到京城。此时，张九龄由一名穷书生成为驸马，同时与双亲再次相见，真是喜上加喜。

So Zhang asked his chef to make a dish that featured auspiciousness and festivals. Accordingly, the chef made four braised meatballs in gravy sauce. When Zhang saw this dish, he asked the chef what it implied. The chef immediately replied, "This dish is called *siyuan* (Four-Round Meatballs). One ball represents your success in the palace examination; the second ball represents the completeness of your wedding; the third ball represents you as the emperor's son-in-law; and the fourth ball represents your family reunion." After hearing that, Zhang repeatedly applauded. He said, "The *siyuan* doesn't sound as good as *sixi* (Four Happiness). Why not name it *sixi wan* (Four-Happiness Meatballs)?" From then on, Four-Happiness Meatballs have become an essential food at wedding feasts.

于是，他便让大厨制作一道吉祥加喜庆的菜肴，厨师做了四个红烧丸子。张九龄看见这道菜，便问厨师这道菜有什么寓意。大厨应声答道："这道菜为'四圆'菜品。一圆金榜题名，二圆成家完婚，三圆做了乘龙快婿，四圆合家团圆。"张九龄听了后，连声称好，说："'四圆'不如叫'四喜'，何不叫'四喜丸'呢？"此后，四喜丸子成了婚宴上必不可少的菜品。

There are several sayings about the meaning of *sixi* (Four Happiness). For example, the traditional *sixi* symbolizes good luck, wealth, longevity, and happiness. It is also said that *sixi* refers to the following four happy events: (1) A good rain comes after a long drought; (2) One's name is put on the published list of successful candidates; (3) The wedding night; (4) Meeting an old friend in an alien land. Nowadays, there is another saying about *sixi*, which refers to wealth, health, harmony, and happiness. No matter what *sixi* means, the four big meatballs remind us to appreciate what we have today.

关于"四喜"的含义，有几种说法。一种是，传统的四喜为福、禄、寿、喜。也有人说，"四喜"为四件喜事：一、久旱逢甘雨；二、金榜题名；三、洞房花烛夜；四、他乡遇故人。如今，"四喜"还有一种说法，即指富裕、健康、和睦、愉快。不论何种说法，四喜丸子都能够唤起我们要珍惜今天所拥有的生活。

56 Baiyun Trotter, a Historically-Known Specialty in Guangzhou 广州历史名菜：白云猪手

Baiyun Trotter is one of the famous dishes in Guangzhou. The following is a way of what this dish is made. Wash the trotters, cut them into pieces and well-cook them; after that, rinse the cooked trotters with running spring water for a day, and then take them out and boil them again with white vinegar, sugar and salt; cool the cooked trotters and soak them in the seasonings for a few hours, and finally serve. As the spring water comes from the Baiyun Hill, the trotters are known as *baiyun zhushou* (Baiyun Trotter or Sweet-and-Sour Trotter).

白云猪手是广州历史名菜之一。这道菜的做法是：洗净猪手，切块，煮熟；再用流动的泉水漂洗一天，捞起后放进加了白醋、白糖和盐的水中煮沸；冷却并浸泡数小时后即可食用。因泉水取自白云山，故名“白云猪手”。

It is said that there was a temple in ancient times on the Baiyun Hill. One day, an old monk in the temple went down to beg for alms. In the temple, there was a little monk who got a trotter. He went out of the temple and found an earthen vessel. There he built an oven to cook the trotter. Soon after the trotter was well cooked, the old monk came back. The little monk was afraid that the old monk would see the cooked trotter, so he hurriedly threw the trotter into the stream at the foot of the hill.

相传，古时白云山上有一座寺院。一天，寺里的老僧下山去了。寺里有个小僧，弄到一只猪手。于是，他出了山门，找了一个土瓦坛，就地垒灶烧煮。猪手煮好后不久，老僧回来了。小僧害怕老僧看见煮熟的猪手，慌忙将猪手扔进山脚下的小溪里。

The next day, a woodman went up the hill to collect firewood. As he passed by the stream, he saw the trotter in the water. He took it home, where he added spices like sugar, salt, and vinegar. The soaked trotter had a crispy skin, and it tasted sweet and sour, fat yet not greasy. The method of cooking trotters soon circulated in the local region. Since this food originated at the foot of the Baiyun Hill, it was later called Baiyun Trotter.

第二天，有个樵夫上山打柴，路过山溪，看到了水里的猪手，就拿回家里，给猪手加了糖、盐、醋等调味料。浸泡后的猪手皮爽脆，吃起来酸中带甜，肥而不腻。不久，这种烹煮猪手的方法便在当地流传开来。由于这种做法源自白云山下，后人便把这个菜肴称作“白云猪手”。

57 The Origins of the Fo Tiaoqiang Food
佛跳墙的由来

Fo tiaoqiang (Buddha Jumping over the Wall) is an unusual name of an assorted stockpot in Fuzhou of Fujian Province. It contains up to 30 ingredients, such as chicken, ham, pork, scallops, abalone, vegetables, and seasonings. The stockpot originated in the late Qing Dynasty and was known as *tanshao babao* (Braised Eight Delicacies in the Jar). Later, it was renamed *fu shou quan* (Full Happiness and Longevity), but it eventually came to be known as the Fo Tiaoqiang Food. One thing should be mentioned that the characters of *fo tiao qiang* are pronounced almost the same as *fu shou quan* in Fuzhou dialect.

佛跳墙之名非同一般，是福建省福州的汤罐，原料多达30种，如鸡肉、火腿、猪肉、扇贝、鲍鱼、蔬菜以及各种佐料。汤罐起源于晚清，名叫“坛烧八宝”，后又改名“福寿全”，最终称为“佛跳墙”。值得一提的是，福州方言里的“佛跳墙”和“福寿全”发音颇为相近。

There are several versions concerning the origin of Fo Tiaoqiang Food. According to one version, a long time ago, there was a little monk in a Buddhist temple. One day, when the little monk was eating meat secretly, an old monk appeared in front of him. Immediately, the little monk ran away and jumped over the temple wall with his meat jar.

关于佛跳墙的由来，有好几种说法。说法一：很久以前，某寺院里有一个小僧。一天，小僧正在偷吃肉时，一个老僧突然出现在他的面前。小僧立刻拿着肉罐跳过了寺院围墙，跑掉了。

In accordance with the second version, there was once a beggar who used a broken earthen jar to beg along streets. When he received some leftover food and wine from restaurants, he put everything into his jar and re-cooked them in the street. A delicious smell wafted up from his cooking jar. A monk sniffed it and couldn't resist the unusual smell. So he jumped out of the temple wall and ate the food to his heart's content. A restaurant owner had his chef prepare the food just like what the beggar did. The chef did it. In addition, he added some other ingredients and cooking wine to enrich the flavor of the dish.

说法二：从前有一个乞丐，拿着破瓦罐沿街乞讨。他从餐馆讨来剩余食物和酒，将其倒入瓦罐，当街重新烧煮。香味从烧煮的瓦罐溢出，一个僧人闻到了，不同寻常的气味让他无法抗拒。他跳墙而出，尽情地吃着这些食物。一家餐馆的老板让厨师像那个乞丐一样烹制这道菜，厨师照此办理，还添加了一些其他配料和料酒，以丰富菜肴的味道。

According to the third version, this food was originally prepared by the wife of an official who worked in the Finance Bureau of Fuzhou in the Qing Dynasty. Once she prepared a family dinner for a senior official invited by her husband. She simmered a stockpot over a low temperature. In the pot, there were chicken, duck, pork, and some seafood. The guest raved about the food prepared by the official's wife. Later, Zheng Chunfa, the chef of the official, learned how to cook this food. He opened his own restaurant and renamed this food *fu shou quan* (Full Happiness and Longevity). He even listed it as the first dish in his restaurant. One scholar wrote down two lines of poetry while eating in the restaurant: "When I open the jar, the delicious meat smell wafts up to everyone near; A monk abandons his deep meditation and jumps over the wall to see what is cooking here." As a result, the food was renamed the Fo Tiaoqiang Food.

说法三：这道菜最初是清代福州官钱局一名官员的夫人烹制的。一次，她主厨家宴，款待丈夫邀请的客人。夫人煨炖汤罐，里面有鸡、鸭、猪肉和几种海鲜。客人对她做的饭菜赞不绝口。后来，衙厨郑春发学会了这道菜，他开设了自己的餐馆，将这道菜命名为"福寿全"，甚至将其列为餐馆的第一道菜。一名在餐馆用餐的文人写下了两行诗："坛启荤香飘四邻，佛闻弃禅跳墙来。"由此，这道菜又改名为"佛跳墙"。

58 The Hotpot, a Unique Cuisine with a Long History 历史悠久的特色美食：火锅

Hotpot (*huoguo*) is a very popular way of eating all over the country; and it can be found wherever there are street-side food stands or small restaurants. Diners gather around a small boiling wok filled with nutritious soup base. Around the wok are placed numerous plates of paper-thin slices of raw meat and other ingredients. The diners select the raw ingredients and boil them in the soup. And then they take them out of the wok and dip them in a small bowl of special sauce before eating.

火锅是国内非常流行的一种饮食方式，在街边小吃摊或小餐馆里随处可见。顾客们围在沸腾的小锅旁，锅里盛满了营养丰富的汤卤。锅的四周放着一盘盘各种薄如纸的生肉片和其他配料。顾客们选好食材，放入汤卤煮沸，然后从锅里夹出食物，蘸上小碗中的特制酱汁，然后食用。

Hotpot is a special food with a long history. *Huodou* is an unearthed iron object used for cooking. This object, which dates back to the Eastern Han Dynasty and is shaped like a basin, is believed to be a type of hotpot-wok. In the Song Dynasty, the cooking method of hotpot was popular among ordinary people. Lin Hong of the Southern Song Dynasty in his cookbook *The Pure Supply at Mountain Home* recorded a story about eating hotpot with his friends. In the Yuan Dynasty, hotpot was introduced to the regions of present-day Mongolia, where the hotpot-wok was used to cook beef and mutton. In the Qing Dynasty, hotpot was not only popular among ordinary people, but also became a famous palace delicacy.

火锅是一种历史悠久的特色美食。"鐎斗"是用于煮食的出土铁器。此物为东汉文物，形如大盆，即为火锅。宋朝，火锅的食法在民间已常见，南宋林洪的《山家清供》食谱中，便有与友人食火锅的介绍。元朝，火锅流传到了当今蒙古一带，用来煮牛羊肉。清朝，火锅不仅在民间盛行，而且成了一道著名的宫廷菜。

There are many kinds of hotpot from all over the country, such as the Seafood Hotpot in Guangdong and Guangxi, the Mutton Hotpot in Beijing, and the Meat Hotpot with Assorted Ingredients in Shanghai. Yuanyang Hotpot is an innovative Sichuan hotpot. The term *yuanyang* refers to things that come in pairs. The wok of the Yuanyang Hotpot is partitioned into two parts, with a thin copper wall in the middle. One part is filled with a hot, spicy soup base, and the other with a light broth. This kind of hotpot was originally prepared by the Chongqing chefs for the First National Cooking Competition in 1983. At that time, it was named by Yan Wenjun as the Double-Flavor Hotpot. In 1985,

Xiong Sizhi changed the name of the Double-Flavored Hotpot to the Yuanyang Hotpot, and the latter has a richer cultural connotation and dietary taste.

全国各地的火锅各具特色，如两广的海鲜火锅、北京的涮羊肉火锅、上海的什锦火锅。而鸳鸯火锅，却是四川创新火锅。鸳鸯比喻“成双配对的事物”。这种火锅用薄铜片把锅子隔成两部分，一边放红汤卤，一边放清汤卤。它最初是为1983年重庆队参加全国第一届烹饪大赛准备的，当时由阎文俊命名为“双味火锅”。1985年，熊四智把“双味火锅”改名为“鸳鸯火锅”，更富有文化韵味和饮食情趣。

The Yuanyang Hotpot has a unique taste. Its wok is an innovative combination of light broth and traditional Sichuan spicy soup and friends or families with different tastes can huddle around and enjoy the exquisite food.

鸳鸯火锅风味别致，巧妙地将清汤火锅与四川传统的红汤火锅汇于一锅。这样，喜好不同味道的朋友或家人可以聚在一起，享受精美的食物。

59 The Origin of the Boiled Blood Curd
毛血旺的由来

The Boiled Blood Curd (*mao xuewang*) is a famous specialty in Chongqing and Sichuan. Its main ingredient is duck blood, and its taste is hot and spicy. So what is the origin of the Boiled Blood Curd?

毛血旺为一道巴蜀名菜，以鸭血为主料，口味属麻辣味。那么，毛血旺是怎么来的呢？

In the Shapingba area west of Chongqing, there is an ancient town by the name of Ciqikou, where its water wharf remains as an important collecting and distributing center along the lower reaches of the Jialing River. There, moored boats and vessels are numerous like a forest, streets are bustling, shops are lively, and merchants are crowded.

在重庆以西的沙坪坝，有一古镇，名磁器口，其水码头历来是嘉陵江下游的物资重要集散地。在那里，系泊在码头的舟楫如林，街道热闹，店铺兴旺，商贾云集。

Seventy years ago, there was a butcher surnamed Wang at the water wharf. Every day after he sold out meat, he would start selling the entrails at low prices. Wang's wife Zhang thought the sale of the entrails at low prices was a waste. Therefore, she set up a street stall, selling soup stewed with shredded entrails including bones, lungs, intestines, and the ingredients such as ginger, Chinese prickly ash, cooking wine, and peas.

七十年前，水码头有位王姓屠夫。每天，他卖完肉后，都会把剩下的下水低价卖掉。王的媳妇姓张，她觉得低价卖掉很可惜。于是，她在街边支起小摊，卖起了炖汤，杂碎汤里有猪骨、肺、肥肠等，辅以姜、麻椒、料酒、豌豆等佐料。

Once by chance, Zhang put fresh blood curd directly into the soup of shredded entrails. She found that the more the blood curd was stewed, the tenderer and tastier it became. It is said that this is the origin of the Boiled Blood Curd, hence the name of *mao xuewang*. *Mao* is Chongqing dialect, meaning "coarse" and "crude." *Xuewang* refers to "blood curd."

一次偶然的机会，张氏把新鲜的猪血旺放入杂碎汤里，他发现血旺越煮越嫩，味道更鲜，遂取名“毛血旺”。“毛”是重庆方言，就是“粗糙”的意思，“血旺”就是“血豆腐”。

60 Zhu Yuanzhang and the Origin of Four Dishes and a Bowl of Soup
四菜一汤与朱元璋

According to legend, in the early Ming Dynasty, the common people all over the country lived in poverty due to natural disasters and poor harvests. However, high officials and noble families continued to enjoy luxurious life.

据传，明朝初年，由于自然灾害和作物歉收，全国各地的百姓生活艰难，而达官贵人却过着奢侈的生活。

One day, it was the birthday of the empress. All the government ministers and officials attended the celebration. When they were all seated, Emperor Zhu Yuanzhang ordered food to be served. The first course was the Stir-Fried Turnip, the second was the Stir-Fried Leeks, the third and fourth courses were two large bowls of green vegetables, and the last course was a bowl of tofu soup with chopped green onions.

一日，皇后寿辰，文武群臣皆到场祝寿。众人就座后，皇帝朱元璋便吩咐上菜。第一道菜是炒萝卜，第二道菜是炒韭菜，第三、四道菜是两大碗青菜，最后是葱花豆腐汤。

Emperor Zhu entertained his guests with vegetarian food, deliberately exhorting all the participants to live a frugal life. After dinner, the emperor announced a rule. He said, “From now on, no meal for guests will be more than four dishes and a bowl of soup. This birthday banquet has set a good example. Those who break the rule will be severely punished without mercy."

朱元璋用家常饭菜款待客人，有心向到场者倡导要生活简朴。晚宴结束后，他宣布一条规定，说："今后请客，最多只能'四菜一汤'，这次皇后的寿筵即是榜样。谁若违反，严惩不贷。"

Later, the established practice of Four Dishes and a Bowl of Soup was spread from the palace to nongovernmental circles. In the middle and late period of the Qing Dynasty, people tended to pursue a luxurious life. At that time, some people of insight proposed treating guests with Four Dishes and a Bowl of Soup. However, the Qing-styled four dishes usually consisted of two dishes of meat and two dishes of vegetables. The meat dishes might be the Steamed Chicken with Rice Flour, Braised Carp, Fried Sliced Pork, or Scrambled Eggs.

后来，"四菜一汤"的规矩便从宫廷传到民间。清朝中后期，人们开始追求奢华的生活。当时，一些有识之士建议用"四菜一汤"宴请客人。然而，清代四菜通常是"两荤两素"，荤菜可能是粉蒸鸡、烧鲫鱼、炒肉片或炒鸡蛋。

第三章
小吃调料文化
Part Three: Snacks and Seasonings

61 Goubuli Steamed Stuffed Buns
狗不理包子

Goubuli Steamed Stuffed Buns (*baozi*) are a specialty in Tianjin. This steamed bun is stuffed with pork, spices and gravy. Also, you can eat these buns with special fillings, such as chicken, shrimp or vegetables. What is more, Goubuli Steamed Stuffed Buns aren't greasy. However, does *goubuli* mean "dogs won't touch them" or "dog doesn't care"? The following is perhaps the most satisfying explanation.

狗不理包子是天津的风味名点。包子馅料为猪肉、调味料、肉汁，还有其他馅料，如鸡肉馅、虾肉馅或美味的素菜馅。此外，狗不理包子还不油腻。然而，"狗不理"的意思令人费解，也许以下的解释是最令人满意的。

In 1831, Gao Guiyou, founder of Goubuli Steamed Stuffed Buns, was born in Xiazhu Village of Wuqing in Tianjin. His father was already forty years old when he was born. So his father call him "Dog Son," hoping that he would be raised as easily as a puppy.

1831年，狗不理包子创始人高贵友出生在天津武清的下朱庄村。其父四十得子，给他取名“狗子”，期望他能像小狗一样好养活。

When Gao Guiyou was fourteen years old, he worked as a young worker in Liu's steamed food shop at the side of the canal south of Tianjin. Gao was ingenious, diligent and curious. Day by day, under the guidance of his master, he constantly improved the skill of *baozi* making.

高贵友十四岁时，到天津南运河边上的刘家蒸吃铺做小伙计。高贵友心灵手巧、刻苦勤奋、求知欲很强。日复一日，在师傅的指导下，他不断地提高包子制作技艺。

Three years after his apprenticeship, Gao himself opened a snack shop of his own, called Deju Hao Eatery, which sold only steamed stuffed buns. Because of Gao's superb skill, his steamed stuffed buns were soft and tasty, and they were not greasy. In addition, his buns were shaped like chrysanthemums. As a result, his business flourished, and more and more people came to eat.

三年学徒期满后，高贵友自己开了一家专营包子的小吃铺，取名“德聚号”。由于高贵友手艺好，包的包子形似菊花，绵软可口，又不油腻，其生意由此兴隆起来，越来越多的人来吃他做的包子。

Under this circumstance, Gao became so busy that he had no time to greet customers. So those who ate his buns joked with him, saying, "Dog Son (his baby name) sells steamed stuffed buns and doesn't care about his customers at all." As time went by, people became accustomed to calling him *goubuli* (Dog doesn't care), while his buns were also known as Goubuli

Steamed Stuffed Buns, and the name of the original shop was gradually ignored.

在这种情况下，高贵友忙得顾不上招呼食客。于是，吃包子的人与他开玩笑说："狗子卖包子，不理人了。"久而久之，人们都习惯地叫他"狗不理"，而他做的包子也被称为"狗不理包子"，而原店铺号却渐渐被人们淡忘了。

Unexpectedly, this special name made his business even more prosperous and Gobuli Steamed Stuffed Buns eventually became a famous traditional Chinese snack. It is said that Yuan Shikai presented the buns as a tribute to Empress Dowager Cixi. She tasted one and praised it effusively. Since then, the reputation of Goubuli Steamed Stuffed Buns grew rapidly, and Gao's branches were gradually established in many places.

出人意料的是，这个特殊名称竟使他的生意更加红火，这个食品最终成为中国著名的传统风味点心。据说，袁世凯曾将狗不理包子作为贡品献给慈禧太后。慈禧太后尝后大悦，大加称赞。从那时起，狗不理包子名声大增，其分号也逐渐在多地设立。

62 The Original Name of Yipin Steamed Stuffed Buns 一品包子的原名

In Kaifeng of Henan Province, there is a snack known as Yipin Steamed Stuffed Buns. Its has a thin layer on the surface, and its meat stuffing is tasty. Originally, it was called Taixue Steamed Buns in the Song Dynasty. *Taixue* was an imperial college, the highest institution of learning in the capital city of ancient China.

河南开封有一种小吃，称"一品包子"。这种包子皮薄，肉馅味美可口。最初的一品包子在宋代叫"太学馒头"。太学指我国古代在京城的最高学府。

As early as the Northern Song Dynasty, Emperor Shen Zong rigorously carried out reforms in order to enrich the country and strengthen his military power. At the same time, the emperor recruited talented men from all over the country to study at the imperial college, stipulating that academically successful scholars could begin their official careers soon after graduation.

早在北宋年间，神宗皇帝厉行变法，以求富国强兵。与此同时，皇帝广招全国各地的人才入太学学习，成绩优秀者可直接进入仕途。

In addition, the emperor himself often visited the imperial college to show his concern for the students. One day, the emperor came to the imperial college again. This time, he asked about the students' diet and wanted to see what was served to them. On that day, the college served the students with steamed stuffed buns. The emperor tasted one and said, "I cannot feel upset when the students are treated with this."

除此之外，神宗还经常亲自视察太学，以表示自己对人才的重视。一次，他问起学生的饮食，要看看他们的饮食如何。那天，学校供应给学生的是包子，神宗尝了尝，便说道："以此养士，可无愧矣！"

From then on, the reputation of the college's steamed stuffed buns quickly spread. Whenever college students returned home to visit their parents, they always brought the buns with them in the hope that their relatives and friends would eat the same buns that once pleased the emperor. Later, people called this food Taixue Steamed Stuffed Buns.

从那时起，太学包子很快出名了。太学生们归家省亲时，总要带太学包子回家乡，希望亲朋好友也能够尝到皇帝夸赞的包子。后来，人们称此食物为“太学包子”。

In the Ming Dynasty, Zhu Su, the fifth son of Zhu Yuanzhang, was crowned with the title of the King of Zhou. He built his residential palace in Kaifeng, where he liked eating Taixue Steamed Stuffed Buns. When princes and court ministers visited Kaifeng, he often treated them with the buns. Zhu was a vassal king, whose status was equivalent to that of the first-rank official in the Ming imperial court. The words “first rank” are “一品” (*yipin*) in Chinese. So, of course, the locals renamed Taixue Steamed Stuffed Buns Yipin Steamed Stuffed Buns.

明代，朱元璋的五皇子朱橚被封为周王。朱橚在开封建起了王府。在那里，他喜欢吃“太学包子”，而且还常常用它来招待来访开封的王公大臣。朱橚身为藩王，其地位相当于朝廷的一品大员，因而当地人就把“太学包子”更名为“一品包子”。

63 The Folk Story About Yangyanr Steamed Stuffed Buns 羊眼儿包子的传说

Yangyanr Steamed Stuffed Buns are a famous snack of the Hui cuisine. *Yangyanr* means “the sheep's eyes.”

羊眼儿包子是回民饮食中的名小吃。“羊眼儿”在英文中就是 the sheep’s eyes。

According to legend, Emperor Kangxi of the Qing Dynasty once dressed in ordinary clothes and walked out of his residential palace to taste Yangyanr Steamed Stuffed Buns. The emperor entered a food shop that sold Hui-style mutton steamed buns. The hospitable shopkeeper served tea to the emperor and said with a smile, “I'm afraid that you won't be satisfied with the food I have to serve. What delicacies have you not tasted in your residential palace? How could you descend from your superior dignity into my humble shop, just for Yangyanr Steamed Stuffed Buns? Honestly, I dare not present the buns."

相传，清朝康熙皇帝一次微服出宫，去品尝羊眼儿包子。当皇帝走进一家回民风味羊肉包子铺时，殷勤的回民掌柜给皇帝上了茶，笑道："如若呈上的饭菜您不满，小的将至感不安。您在宫廷什么美食没尝过，敢烦屈驾到卑下铺子，只为尝羊眼儿包子，小的实在不敢敬上。"

The emperor was aware that the shopkeeper already knew his identity, but he remained at ease, insisting that he would prefer to eat Yangyanr Steamed Stuffed Buns here.

康熙皇帝明知自己的身份已被识破，但还是举止轻松自若，执意要在此吃羊眼儿包子。

The shopkeeper said, "Your presence in my humble shop is my great honor. Just a moment, please, and the buns will be ready soon."

掌柜说，"蒙您照拂卑下铺子，不胜荣幸。请稍等，包子马上就好了。"

A few minutes later, the shopkeeper returned with a plate of hot steamed buns. The emperor picked up a bun with his chopsticks and put it into his mouth to taste it. He was very pleased with the bun's good smell, delicious taste, and excellent ingredients.

不一会儿，掌柜便端来了一盘热腾腾的包子。康熙皇帝用筷子夹了一个包子，放到嘴里尝了尝。喷香的包子味道鲜美，配料精细，皇帝大悦。

"Where are the sheep's eyes in the bun?" the emperor asked.
"包子的羊眼儿呢？" 康熙皇帝问道。

The shopkeeper replied, "The meat filling in the buns has no sheep's eyes at all. The size of each bun is small, and I made them into the shape of the sheep's eyes, so people called them Yangyanr Steamed Stuffed Buns."
掌柜答道："肉馅里根本就没有羊眼儿。包子个头都很小，我把它们做成了羊眼睛的形状，所以称为'羊眼儿包子'。"

"Your buns are tasty. Please send them to my residential palace at regular intervals," said the emperor.
皇帝道："包子可口好吃，可常送入宫中。"

Since then, Yangyanr Steamed Stuffed Buns gained considerable fame all over the capital city. As a result, other Hui people followed suit and made steamed buns in the same shape. Gradually Yangyanr Steamed Stuffed Buns became one of the favorite snacks among them.
从此，羊眼儿包子声名大噪，誉满京城。于是，其他回民也纷纷效仿，做起同样形状的包子，这个食品遂成了回民喜爱的小吃之一。

64 Zhuge Liang and Crab-Roe Soup Buns 蟹黄汤包与诸葛亮

Crab-Roe Soup Buns are a traditional snack in Jiangsu Province. Making the bun is quite an art. The bun fillings mainly include crab roe, crab meat, and pure chicken soup.
蟹黄汤包是江苏传统小吃，制作工艺精妙，其馅主要是蟹黄、蟹肉和原味鸡汤。

According to legend, early in the Three Kingdoms Period there existed Crab-Roe Soup Buns. Toward the late Three Kingdoms Period, Zhuge Liang became seriously ill, and he remembered the marriage between his first lord Liu Bei and Sun Shangxiang, General Sun Quan's sister. At that time, Liu Bei went to the Kingdom of Wu to participate in his own wedding ceremony. Not long after his wedding, Liu Bei left the Kingdom of Wu, but his newly married wife Sun Shangxiang didn't follow him because Sun Quan forced her to stay in Wu. Day and night, Sun missed her husband Liu Bei, who was far away. Later, Liu Bei died of illness in Baidi City. At the news of his death, Sun grieved deeply. She climbed up to the Lingyun Pavilion on Beigu Mountain, where she mourned for her husband and then threw herself into the river. At that time, Zhuge Liang was so busy with battle affairs that he himself had no time to go to the Kingdom of Wu to mourn for Sun's death.

传说早在三国时期，就有了蟹黄汤包。三国后期，诸葛亮病重时，想到先主刘备与孙权将军妹妹孙尚香的一桩婚事。当时，刘备赴东吴参加婚礼。成婚后不久，刘备便离开东吴，但他的新婚夫人孙尚香却没有随他离开，因为孙权强行把她留在吴国。孙夫人日夜思念远在他乡的丈夫刘备。后来，刘备在白帝城病逝。听闻刘备病逝，孙夫人非常悲痛。她登上北固山凌云亭，祭奠刘备后投江自尽。当时，诸葛亮忙于战事，未能顾上到东吴哀悼亡灵。

When Zhuge Liang recalled what had happened in the past, he decided to send someone to the Kingdom of Wu to pay homage to the late Sun so as to realize his original intention. So Zhuge

Liang called Old Wu and ordered him to go to the Kingdom of Wu on this mission. Old Wu was a military attaché who had once followed Liu Bei into that region. He asked what he would take to the memorial service. Zhuge Liang said that steamed buns with meat filling would do.

当诸葛亮想起往事，就决定派人去东吴祭奠已故的孙夫人，以了却自己的心愿。于是，诸葛亮就召唤了吴老头，令他去东吴执行此次使命。吴老头是一名尉役，曾经跟随刘备去过那里。他问带什么物品去祭奠，诸葛亮说用肉馒头祭奠。

Old Wu followed what Zhuge Liang said. He sailed to the Kingdom of Wu, where he told a local magistrate that he came to hold a memorial service for the late Sun. Hearing this, the magistrate did not dare to neglect Old Wu and arranged him to stay in a guest house.

吴老头听从吩咐，便乘船来到东吴，禀告当地知府说是来祭奠已故的孙夫人的。知府一听，不敢怠慢，便安排吴老头住在驿馆。

Once settled in the guest house, Old Wu began to knead dough with wheat flour, chop pork, and prepare seasonings. He remembered that crabs had been Sun's favorite food. So he cooked some crabs and removed the crab roe and meat out of the shells. He then mixed the minced pork and seasonings with the crab roe and meat to make the filling.

吴老头住下后，便揉面，剁猪肉，准备佐料。这时，他又想起孙夫人在世时最喜欢吃螃蟹。于是，他又煮了一些螃蟹，剥出蟹黄和蟹肉，然后把蟹黄、蟹肉、猪肉馅和佐料搅拌起来，做成了馅心。

The next day, Old Wu and his entourage came to the

riverside at the foot of the Beigu Mountain, where they set up an incense table, burned the incense and candles, and placed 49 steamed meat buns on the table. Then, Old Wu read the eulogy written by Zhuge Liang and threw the buns into the river.

第二天，吴老头一行来到北固山脚下的河边，摆上香案，点燃香烛，案桌上摆放四十九个肉馒头。然后，吴老头宣读诸葛亮写的祭文，并把包子抛入江里。

After the memorial service, everyone asked Old Wu what he had just thrown into the river. Old Wu smiled. He said mysteriously that this was Madam Sun's favorite food in her lifetime, and it was called *xiehuang tàngbao* (crab-roe hot buns). As Old Wu lost several teeth, he couldn't pronounce some words distinctly. For the word "烫" (*tàng*, hot), he pronounced it "汤" (*tāng*, soup). "烫" and "汤" have the same sound, but they have different tones, which leads to different meanings. However, everyone mistakenly assumed "烫" (*tàng*, hot) to be the word "汤" (*tāng*, soup), and thus the name of the food *xiehuang tāngbao* (Crab-Roe Soup Buns) spread.

祭奠结束后，大家问吴老头刚才扔进河里的是什么。吴老头笑了笑，故弄玄虚地说，这是孙夫人生前最喜爱吃的食物，是"蟹黄烫包"。吴老头掉了几颗牙，吐字有点不清，把"烫"字读成了"汤"。"烫"和"汤"音似，但声调不一样，意思也不同。然而，众人却误认为"烫"就是"汤"，于是便有了"蟹黄汤包"这个名字。

65 The Origin of the Chinese Dumplings 饺子的由来

In October 1978, archaeologists excavated a king's tomb

in the ruins of the former capital of the State of Xue (present-day Tengzhou County of Shandong Province). The State of Xue was a small kingdom in the Late Spring and Autumn Period.

1978年10月，考古工作者在今山东省滕州的薛国故城发掘了一座薛国君主墓。薛国是春秋晚期的诸侯小国。

Among the unearthed copper sacrificial vessels, there was a rusty food container. The archaeologists opened it and found some white food neatly placed inside. The food was triangular in shape, each being 5 to 6 centimeters long, and 3.5 to 4 centimeters wide at its widest point. Judging by the shape and what was inside, they believed that this food should be dumplings. However, they did not reveal what kind of dumpling fillings eaten by the tomb owner.

在出土的铜制礼器中，有一个锈蚀的铜制食器。考古工作者打开一看，只见里面整齐地放着一些白色食物，呈三角形，每个长5至6厘米，最宽处3.5至4厘米。考古工作者从食物的形状和里面包裹的馅料看，认为这种食物应该是饺子。然而，他们并没有透露墓主吃的是哪种饺子馅。

According to *Guang Ya* (one of China's earliest encyclopedias) written by Zhang Yi of the Kingdom of Wei in the Three Kingdoms Period, there was a kind of food called wonton, which looked like a crescent moon and was roughly similar to today's dumplings. During the Southern and Northern Dynasties, dumplings "shaped like a crescent moon and were available all over the country." It is said that they were served in a bowl with soup at that time. Around the Tang Dynasty, dumplings became exactly the same as today's *jiaozi*, and they were served on plates, without soup.

据三国魏人张揖著的《广雅》记载，那时有一种叫“馄饨”的食品，形如月牙，和现在的饺子形状基本相似。南北朝时期，馄饨“形如偃月，天下通食”。据说，那时的饺子盛在碗里和汤一起吃。大约在唐代，饺子和现在的饺子一模一样，而且放在无汤的盘里吃。

In ancient times, there were a number of different names for dumplings, including *laowan*, *fenjiao*, *bianshi* and *jiao'er*. Nowadays, in the north, this food is called *jiaozi*; in many areas of the south, it is named wonton. In addition, dumplings can be stuffed with a variety of foods, including pork, mutton, beef, fish, as well as the three delicacies.

古时饺子有若干不同的名称，如:“牢丸”“粉角”“扁食”“饺耳”。现在，在北方，这种食物称为“饺子”，而在南方的许多地区却称为“馄饨”。此外，饺子的馅料多种多样，包括猪肉、羊肉、牛肉、鱼肉、三鲜等。

There are several versions about the origin of dumplings. According to one version, they were invented by Zhang Zhongjing, a well-known herbalist of the Eastern Han Dynasty.

饺子的来历有几种说法。根据说法一，饺子是由东汉著名的草药医生张仲景发明的。

When Zhang resigned from government office and returned to his hometown, he found that many local people had painful frostbite on their ears in winter. Zhang realized that his clinic might be too small to accommodate the increasing number of frostbite patients, so he asked his brother to put up a tent and place a cauldron on the village ground.

张仲景辞官还乡后，他发现当地很多人的耳朵在冬天患了冻疮，异常疼痛。他觉得自己的诊所可能太小了，无法容纳越来越多的冻疮患者，于是，就让自己的兄长在村里的空地上搭起帐篷，支起大锅。

When the winter solstice arrived, Zhang started to offer medicinal herbs to frostbite patients. His medicine, known as *quhan jiao'er tang* (herbal soup to dispel the cold), was made of mutton, red spicy pepper, and other necessary herbs. Zhang soaked them completely in water and then heated them in the cauldron over a fire until the water came to a boil. After that, Zhang took all the things out of the pot and minced them to make the filling. His assistants rolled out dough into dough wrappers, each shaped like a small pancake. They put each wrapper in the palm of their hands, and then placed the filling in the center and wrapped the food in the shape of an ear. These tiny things, called *jiao'er* or "the charming ear," were all dropped into the herb soup to cook. Zhang gave each patient a bowl of the soup and two *jiao'er* dumplings. The patients drank the soup and ate *jiao'er*, and they soon felt warm even to their ears.

冬至到来时，张仲景就专门舍药为患者治疗冻伤。他的药叫"祛寒娇耳汤"，汤里有羊肉、辣椒，以及其他所需的草药。张仲景将它们完全浸泡在水中，然后在火上的大锅里加热，直至水沸腾。最后，他把锅里所有的东西都捞出来，切碎做成馅。他的帮手把面剂擀成一个个像小薄饼的面皮，再把面皮放在掌心，将馅料放在中间包起来，状若耳形。这些食物被称为"娇耳"，皆放入草药汤里煮沸。张仲景给每个病人一碗汤和两个"娇耳"。病人们喝了汤，吃了"娇耳"，顿觉全身甚至两耳都温暖发热。

Over the next few days, as they continued to eat dumplings and drink soup, the frostbite on their ears gradually subsided. Until New Year's Eve, Zhang had been serving the medicinal soup and *jiao'er* dumplings. On the New Year's Day, the locals celebrated the festival by making dumplings and rejoiced over their recovery from the frostbite. This event has gradually evolved into a tradition that continues to this day.

接下来的几天，他们继续吃“娇耳”，喝汤，耳朵冻伤逐渐消退。张仲景一直施舍药汤和“娇耳”，直到大年三十。新年第一天，当地人包“娇耳”庆祝新年，庆贺冻伤康复。这种做法渐渐变成了习俗，一直延续至今。

66 The Old Name of Deep-Fried Twisted Dough Sticks 油条的旧名

The Deep-Fried Twisted Dough Stick, also known as *youtiao* in Chinese, is a traditional snack for breakfast. Initially, it was called *youzha hui*. Its origin is said to be related to Qin Hui, the prime minister during the Jianyan and Shaoxing years of the Southern Song Dynasty.

油条是传统的早餐小吃。最初，油条的名字叫作“油炸桧”。据说，这个小吃的起源与曾任南宋建炎、绍兴年间宰相的秦桧有关。

In the eighth Shaoxing year (1138), Hangzhou was officially designated as the capital city. In the eleventh Shaoxing year (1141), a peace treaty was signed between the Southern Song Dynasty and the State of Jin. The year 1142 brought the death of Yue Fei, a celebrated general of the Southern Song Dynasty. However, the groundless accusation against Yue Fei was a snare secretly set up by Qin Hui and his wife. After hearing of Yue Fei's death, the people in the capital were furious. They hated Qin Hui and his wife so much that they often talked about this matter in restaurants, teahouses, streets, or alleys.

绍兴八年（1138），杭州被正式定为都城。绍兴十一年（1141），南宋与金国订立了和议。1142年，南宋著名将军岳飞遇害。然而，对岳飞的"莫须有"罪名，其实就是秦桧夫妇暗中设下的圈套。都城百姓听到岳飞的死讯后非常愤怒，憎恨秦桧夫妇。他们经常在酒楼茶馆、街头巷尾议论这件事。

At that time, near the place where Yue Fei died, there was a small eatery that mainly sold oil-fried food. The eatery owner was frying food when he heard of Yue Fei's death. Unable to contain his resentment at the terrible news, he took a lump of flour dough from a basin and kneaded it into two small figures — a man and a woman. The owner pasted the two dough figures back-to-back together and threw them into an oil pot. Meanwhile, he repeatedly shouted, "Come and eat deep-fried oil Qin Hui!"

当时，在岳飞去世的附近，有一家以卖油炸食品为主的小食店。一天，小食店掌柜正在油炸食物时突然听到了岳飞的死讯。这个可怕的消息传来后，掌柜难以按捺住心中愤恨，便从面盆里拿起一块面团，揉成了一男一女两个小人儿。他将这两个面人背对背地粘在一起，扔进油锅里，同时一遍又一遍地大声喊着："过来吃油炸秦桧！"

Upon hearing his shouting, people around understood what he was referring to. Soon, they gathered around the basin. They shouted as they ate the fried figures and helped the owner knead more small figures. Other inns and restaurants in the same city quickly followed suit, frying "Qin Hui dough" in the same way as the small eatery did. This practice thus spread widely throughout the country and continued to this day.

周围的人听到他的喊声，心里都明白他的意思。人们很快就围在面盆的周围，一边喊着，一边吃着油炸小人儿，同时帮助掌柜揉捏更多的小人儿。同城的小吃店和餐馆也纷纷效仿，按照小吃店那样的方法油炸“秦桧面团”。这种做法在全国广泛传播，并延续至今。

Nowadays, people prefer to call this food *youtiao* (Deep-Fried Twisted Dough Sticks) rather than *youzha hui* (Oil-Fried Hui). However, in some areas, the locals still use the old name Deep-Fried Hui or Deep-Fried Ghost.

如今，人们更喜欢称这种食品为“油条”，而不叫“油炸桧”。然而，在一些地区，当地人依然使用旧名称“油炸桧”或“油炸鬼”。

67 The Origin of Knife-Sliced Noodles
刀削面的由来

Knife-Sliced Noodles are a kind of wheat-flour food with unique flavor and they are deeply loved by the locals in Shanxi Province. The knife is actually a piece of curved, sharp sheet metal specifically made for making this food. A noodle chef usually holds well-kneaded dough in his left palm and the knife between the fingers of his right hand. At the same time, he/she faces a boiling water pot. The chef then begins to slice the dough horizontally with his/her knife, and the sliced dough flakes leap into the pot. Each flake is about six inches long and triangular in shape. In addition, it is thick in the middle and thin at the edges. The flakes keep rolling up and down in the boiling water, like silvery fish frolicking in a rushing river. A skilled chef can slice as many as 200 dough flakes per minute.

刀削面是一种风味独特的小麦面食，深受山西当地人喜爱。所用之刀，实际上就是弧形、锋利的薄铁片，是为制作这种食物特制的。面条师傅通常左手掌托住揉好的面团，右手指捏着刀片；同时，他们面朝滚开的汤锅，然后平行地用刀削面团，削出的面叶跃入锅中。每片面叶大约六英寸长，呈三角形，中厚边薄。面叶就像银鱼在急流中戏水，不停地在滚烫的汤锅里翻来滚去。一名熟练厨师每分钟刀削面片可以多达二百块。

The origin of Knife-Sliced Noodles can be traced back to ancient times when Mongol cavalry occupied the Central Plains where the Han people lived. In order to prevent the Han rebellion, the Mongol soldiers confiscated all metal tools owned by each household. At the same time, they required that every ten households should share only one kitchen knife; after the knife was used, it needed to be returned to the Mongols for safekeeping.

刀削面的起源可以追溯到古代蒙古族人占领汉人居住的中原地区时。为了防止汉人造反起义，蒙古兵把家家户户的金属工具全部没收，并规定每十户人家公用一把厨刀，用完后再交回来保管。

One day, an old man was preparing noodles for lunch. He went out to fetch the shared kitchen knife to cut the kneaded dough into thin strips of noodles. Unexpectedly, the knife had already been taken away by another family, so he had to return home and wait for his turn.

一天，一位老汉正在为午饭做面条。他出去取共用的厨刀，好把揉好的面团切成细细的面条。不料，刀被另一户人家拿走了，老汉只好返回家，等着轮到自己。

On the way home, the old man saw a thin sheet of iron lying on the ground. He picked it up and hid it under his clothes.

在回家的路上，老汉看见地上有一块薄铁皮，便顺手捡起来揣在怀里。

As soon as the old man got home, he took out the iron sheet and said to himself, "Let me see if I can use this sheet to replace the kitchen knife." He kneaded the dough and sharpened the sheet. After that, he placed the dough in the palm of his left hand and picked up the sheet with his right hand. He began to slice the dough horizontally, and the sliced flakes one after another flew into a pot of boiling water. Soon, the noodles were cooked well.

老汉一到家，就取出那块铁皮，自言自语道："让我看看可否用这块铁皮替代厨刀吧。"他揉好面团，磨了磨那块薄铁皮。然后，他把面团放在左手掌上，右手拿起薄铁皮，开始平行地刀削面团，削出的面叶一个接一个地飞入滚开的汤锅里。很快，面条就做好了。

The old man scooped the sliced flakes out of the pot and ate the noodles with some sauces. "Very good!" he thought, "This iron sheet is perfect. From now on, I don't have to wait in line for the shared kitchen knife."

老汉从锅里捞出刀削面叶，浇上调味汁，便吃起来。"非常好！"老汉想道，"这块薄铁皮很好用。今后，我再也不用排队等那把厨刀了。"

68 The Legend of Crossing-the-Bridge Rice Noodles 过桥米线的传说

Guoqiao mixian literally means "crossing-the-bridge rice noodles." This food is Yunnan's local rice noodles, made with a bowl of hot chicken broth, a bowl of rice noodles, vegetables, and a few slices of raw fish, chicken, and ham. The broth usually remains boiling hot in a bowl for some time. Thinly sliced raw ingredients and rice noodles are heated in the bowl until they are ready to serve.

过桥米线这种食物是云南本地的米线，用一碗热鸡汤、一碗米粉、一些蔬菜以及几片生鱼片、鸡肉和火腿制成。汤汁在碗里通常保持滚烫的温度一段时间，切成薄片的原料和米粉在碗中烫熟后食用。

Crossing-the-Bridge Rice Noodles have a history of more than 100 years. A long time ago, according to legend, there was a lake, which was outside the town of Mengzi in Yunnan. In the middle of the lake there was a scenic islet that stood among green trees, beautiful pavilions, and tall towers. The islet provided a comfortable and appealing place for scholars to escape from town and concentrate on their studies of classics.

过桥米线已经有一百多年的历史。相传很久以前，云南蒙自外有一个湖泊，湖中央有一座风景优美的小岛，岛上绿树掩映着亭台楼阁。这个小岛成了书生们避世、攻读诗书的怡人舒适之地。

At that time, a scholar stayed here to prepare for the imperial civil examination. Every day, his wife brought him food, which she had to carry across a wooden bridge to the islet. The scholar was so absorbed in preparing for his exam that he often neglected to eat his food while it was warm. His preoccupation caused his wife to worry about his health.

当时，有一名书生在这座岛上准备科举考试。他的妻子每天给他送饭。她带着食物，需走过一座木桥，才能到达小岛。书生专心备考，常常忘记趁热吃饭，这让妻子非常担心他因饮食不规律而影响身体健康。

One day, his wife slaughtered a fat chicken and stewed it in a casserole. After cooking, she brought her husband a pot of chicken broth in which she added rice noodles and other ingredients. The broth was covered with chicken fat to prevent heat loss. Unexpectedly, the heat of the rice noodles stayed in the broth for a long time. Besides, the noodles are tasty. Her husband liked this broth, so from that day on, his wife continued to deliver the rice noodles in the same kind of broth.

一天，书生的妻子宰了一只肥鸡，放入砂锅炖了起来。做好后，她给丈夫送来一罐鸡汤，里面还加入了米线和其他配料。鸡汤上面覆盖着鸡油，以防止热量流失。没想到，米线的热温还在汤汁里留存了好一会儿，而且味道还不错，书生非常喜欢这种汤汁。从那天起，他的妻子继续送米线，用的是同样的汤汁。

The scholar succeeded in passing his examination. Later, he often recalled that his wife crossed the bridge and brought him rice noodles in chicken broth every day, so he named this kind of noodles *guoqiao mixian* or Crossing-the-Bridge Rice Noodles.

书生成功地通过了科举考试。后来，他时常回忆起妻子每天过桥送鸡汤米线，故给米线取名叫“过桥米线”。

The story about the scholar and his wife, as well as the new name of the rice noodles, spread throughout the region, so many locals started to follow suit and cook rice noodles as the scholar's wife did. As time went by, people continued improving their cooking methods, thus making Crossing-the-Bridge Rice Noodles widely spread in Yunnan.

书生与他妻子的故事，以及米线的新名称传遍整个地区，当地许多人开始效仿书生妻子做起米线。随着岁月的流逝，人们不断改进烹饪法，这使得“过桥米线”在云南家喻户晓。

69 Records and Versions About Yangzhou Fried Rice 扬州炒饭的记载与说法

Yangzhou Fried Rice, also known as Fried Rice with Egg in Yangzhou, is a traditional super dish in Yangzhou of Jiangsu Province. The main ingredients include rice, ham, eggs, shrimp, and so on.

扬州炒饭，又名扬州蛋炒饭，是江苏扬州的传统美食，主要食材是米饭、火腿、鸡蛋、虾等。

It is said that Emperor Yang Di of the Sui Dynasty liked eating Fried Rice with Egg. He brought this dish into Yangzhou when he was on a cruise in Jiangdu (present-day Yangzhou of Jiangsu).

据说，隋炀帝喜欢吃鸡蛋炒饭。他在巡游江都（今江苏扬州）时，就把鸡蛋炒饭传到这里。

Some scholars believe that Fried Rice with Egg originated from the locals in Yangzhou. According to textual research, as early as the Spring and Autumn Period, this dish was already eaten by boat people sailing along the ancient Hangou Canal of Yangzhou. In the old days of Yangzhou, if there was leftover rice at noon, the supper would be fried rice made with leftover rice, one or two eggs, chopped green onions, and other seasonings.

有学者认为，扬州炒饭源于扬州本地人。据考证，早在春秋时期，航行在扬州古运河邗沟上的船民就食用鸡蛋炒饭。旧时扬州，如果中午有剩饭，那么晚餐就是蛋炒饭，用剩饭、一两个鸡蛋、葱花和其他调味料做成。

In the Ming Dynasty, local chefs in Yangzhou added other ingredients to the fried rice, which initially formed the prototype of Yangzhou Fried Rice. In the Jiaqing Years of the Qing Dynasty, Yi Bingshou, Prefect of Yangzhou, began to add shrimp meat, cubes of lean meat, and ham while frying rice with eggs and onion. Gradually, thanks to his efforts, Yangzhou Fried Rice evolved into a variety of dishes that blended with other ingredients to make it even more palatable. Later, Yi resigned his government post and returned to his hometown in Fujian. In the meantime, he brought back home the recipe. In his book *A Poetry Collection of the Thatched Cottage in the Remaining Spring*, he detailed the cooking methods of the Yangzhou Fried Rice. At that time, this food was not only a Yangzhou-style specialty, but also a delicious food on the Cantonese menu.

明代，扬州本地厨师在炒饭中加入了其他食材，初步形成了扬州炒饭的雏形。清朝嘉庆年间，扬州知府伊秉绶在炒葱花蛋炒饭时开始加入虾仁、瘦肉丁、火腿。此举使扬州炒饭逐渐演变成多种多样的蛋炒饭，由于添加了其他食材，蛋炒饭的味道更为鲜美。后来，伊秉绶辞官回到老家福建。他把扬州炒饭也带了过去，并在他所著的《留春草堂诗钞》中详细地介绍了它的制作方法。这时的扬州炒饭不仅是扬州风味食物，还是粤式菜谱中的一道美食。

70 Empress Dowager Cixi and the Steamed Corn Bread 窝窝头与慈禧太后

The Steamed Corn Bread (*wowotou*) is made with corn flour or corn and bean flour. Each piece of bread has a solid body with a round and flat bottom that gradually narrows toward the top. The center of the bottom is curved inward, allowing steam to easily heat the bread.

窝窝头，是玉米面或玉米和豆面粉混合做成的食物，立体状，圆平底，成圆锥形。底下有窝，易于蒸熟。

There is an interesting story about the Steamed Corn Bread. In 1900, the Eight-Power Allied Forces invaded China. Before the troop moved into Beijing, Empress Dowager Cixi and her palace staffs fled from the capital to the west.

关于窝窝头，有一则有趣的故事。1900年，八国联军入侵中国。联军入京前，慈禧太后和皇宫人员离开了京城，向西逃去。

On the way toward the west, Cixi felt hungry and fatigued. The eunuchs searched everywhere in hope to get food for her. They found nothing, but one cold steamed corn bread from a villager nearby.

在西去的路上，慈禧感到又饿又累。太监们四处寻找，希望为慈禧弄到食物。在附近一个村子里，他们只找到了一块冷窝窝头。

The eunuchs presented the corn bread to Cixi, who picked it up and ate it eagerly. Afterward, she felt comfortable. When Cixi returned to her palace, she had her chefs make corn bread for her. The chefs cooked it in the imperial kitchen. This kind of corn bread was small in shape and was made with refined corn flour, soybean flour, sugar, and osmanthus petals.

太监把窝窝头献给了慈禧，她拿起来，迫不及待地吃了起来，吃完后才感到舒适。慈禧返回宫后，就让厨师为她做窝窝头。厨师们在御膳房做了窝窝头，这种窝窝头比较小，由精制玉米面、豆面、糖和桂花制成。

Cixi really liked it. Later, this corn bread was called *xiao wowotou* (Small Steamed Corn Bread) and became one of the best-known snacks in the imperial kitchen of the Qing Dynasty.

慈禧果然喜欢。后来，人们称这种窝窝头为“小窝窝头”，它成为清朝御膳房最有名的小吃之一。

71 The Legend of Sweet Glutinous Rice Dumplings 元宵的传说

On the 15th day of the first month of the Chinese lunar calendar, every family has the tradition to eat *yuanxiao* (sweet glutinous rice dumplings). These sweet balls, also known as *tangyuan* (sweet balls in soup), symbolize family reunion, affection and happiness.

农历正月十五，家家户户有吃元宵的习俗。甜蜜的元宵，即“汤圆”，象征着家庭的团聚、关爱和幸福。

Folklore tells how people began eating *yuanxiao* during the reign of Emperor Wu Di of the Han Dynasty. One snowy day, Dongfang Shuo, a man of letters and a courtier of the emperor, went to the royal garden to pluck some plum blossoms for His Majesty. As he entered the garden gate, he saw a palace maid with tears streaming down her face and ready to throw herself into a well.

据民间传说，吃元宵始于汉武帝时期。一天，下着雪，文学侍臣东方朔去御花园为皇上折梅花。一进园门，他就看见一名宫女泪流满面，准备投井。

Dongfang rescued her. This palace maid was called Yuanxiao. Since she came to the palace, she had never seen her family. Every year during festival occasions, she was more homesick than usual, and she thought that she would rather die if she couldn't fulfill her filial duty to her parents.

东方朔救了她。这个宫女叫元宵，自从她进宫后，就再也没有与家人见面了。每年节日期间，她就比平常更加思念家人，认为不能在双亲跟前尽孝，不如一死了之。

Dongfang took pity on her and found a way for her to be reunited with her family. He told her to dress herself in red and go into the main street of the capital to read out a statement in the name of the Jade Emperor: "I, the Deity of Fire, have come here under orders of the Jade Emperor to burn down the city of Chang'an. The city is destined to be destroyed; the fire will burn down the imperial palace; on the 15th day of the first lunar month, the midnight sky will be lit up by flames."

东方朔同情她，想到一个能让她与家人团聚的办法。他让元宵身着红色衣裳，到京城大街上，以玉皇大帝的名义宣读圣旨，说："鄙人为火神君，奉玉皇大帝之命来火烧长安。长安在劫，火焚帝阙，十五天火，焰红宵夜。"

The maid did as he said. Dressed in red, she went out into the street, where she read aloud a statement from the Jade Emperor. Those who heard her reading the statement believed it to be true and hastily pleaded with her for mercy. The girl in red replied, "Well, if you really want to avert this disaster, take this written statement to the emperor and let him decide what to do."

宫女按东方朔的吩咐照办。她身着红衣，走到街上，大声地念起玉皇大帝的圣旨。那些听她宣读的人皆信以为真，急忙求她开恩。红衣女子回答道："好吧，若想避免灾难，可将这份圣旨交给皇上，让他决断吧。"

After saying that, the girl in red dropped the imperial edict and walked away. The note was sent to Emperor Wu Di, who read it and was greatly surprised. Immediately, the emperor invited Dongfang to come to the palace for advice. Dongfang said, "I understand the Deity of Fire likes eating sweet glutinous rice dumplings, and the maid Yuanxiao is good at making them. The Deity of Fire may also know that the sweet glutinous rice dumplings made by her are delicious. Your Majesty can order her to make sweet glutinous rice dumplings on the night of the 15th day of the first lunar month. In addition, Your Majesty issues a decree ordering each family in the capital to make this food. During this period, people should burn incense and offer the dumplings as a sacrifice to the Deity of Fire, who will be surely pleased and change his mind. What is more, Your Majesty also asks the people in the capital to make *yuanxiao* lanterns and hung them along the streets and lanes, in courtyards, and on doors. At the same time, they should set off fireworks on the night of the 15th day of the first lunar month as if the whole city were ablaze. So the Jade Emperor will mistake it as the city on fire."

红衣女子说完，便扔下圣旨而去。人们把写着圣旨的帖子送到汉武帝那里。武帝一看，心惊不已，连忙请东方朔进宫出谋献策。东方朔说："听说火神君爱吃汤圆，而宫女元宵擅长做汤圆。火神君也许也知道她做的汤圆可口好吃，皇上可以让元宵在正月十五晚上做好汤圆。此外，皇上传令京都家家做汤圆，同时焚香上供，用汤圆敬奉火神君，这会让火神欣慰不已而改变主意。皇上还要让京城人人做元宵灯笼，挂在大街小巷、院子里、门上，并在元月十五夜燃放烟花，好像满城大火似的，这样就可以瞒过玉皇大帝了。"

After hearing that, the emperor issued a decree based on Dongfang's proposal. So on the 15th day of the first lunar month, many people went into the capital to view the lanterns, and the parents of the maid Yuanxiao were also among them. When they saw big lanterns with "元宵" (*yuanxiao*) written on them, they cried out in surprise, "Yuanxiao! Yuanxiao!" Of course, the maid Yuanxiao heard the cry, and she was finally reunited with her family on that day.

武帝听后，根据东方朔的建议颁布了一道谕旨。于是，在农历正月十五这一天，许多人来到京城看花灯，宫女元宵的父母也在其中。当他们看到写着"元宵"的大灯笼时，便惊奇地叫道："元宵！元宵！"宫女元宵听到了呼喊声，终于在那天与家人团聚了。

Because the sweet rice dumplings made by the maid Yuanxiao were the best, the 15th day of the first lunar month was named the Yuanxiao Festival, and the sweet dumplings were also called *yuanxiao*. Today, the sweet rice dumplings in China have many different flavors. Preparing and eating them during the Yuanxiao Festival is a traditional delight.

因为宫女元宵做的汤圆最好吃，所以正月十五就被命名为元宵节，而汤圆也被称为"元宵"。如今，中国汤圆有许多不同的口味。在元宵节期间，人们习惯做元宵，吃元宵，欣喜快乐。

72 How the Wife Cake Takes Its Name
老婆饼取名缘由

The Wife Cake originated in Chaozhou of Guangdong. It is a baked cake with a golden outer layer and sweet filling. It tastes crispy and is fried in layers, each layer being as thin as cotton paper.

最初，老婆饼来自广东潮州，烤好的饼子外表金黄，内有甜酱馅，吃起来酥脆，层层叠叠，每层薄如绵纸。

According to legend, toward the end of the Qing Dynasty, in Guangzhou there existed a teahouse, which was well known for its various snacks and cakes. In the teahouse bakery, there was a pastry baker who was from Chaozhou. One day, he returned home with various teahouse-baked cakes that his wife loved.

相传，清朝末年，广州有一家茶馆，以制作各种小吃和糕点而闻名。茶馆里的糕饼房，有一位潮州糕点师傅。一天，他带着茶馆烤的各式糕点回到家，给妻子送上她喜欢吃的糕点。

After her wife had tasted all the cakes, she said, “The cakes made in the teahouse are not tasty as I have expected. I’m afraid that the white-gourd cake made by my parents is much better than these cakes.”

他的妻子品尝了带回来的所有糕点后说道：“茶馆所做的糕点并不像我想象的那么好吃，恐怕我父母做的冬瓜角比这些点心还好吃呢。”

Of course, what his wife said did not convince her husband. He asked his wife to make a white-gourd cake for him to taste. So, she made some white-gourd cakes, which looked golden and were filled with sweet gourd paste. After the baker ate it, he couldn't help praising the gourd cake for its sweetness and delicacy.

当然，丈夫不相信妻子说的话，他让妻子做冬瓜角，他要尝尝。于是，她做了些冬瓜角，这种糕点外表金黄，内有甜甜的冬瓜馅。潮州师傅吃过之后，禁不住称赞冬瓜角香甜可口。

The next day, the Chaozhou baker returned to his teahouse with some white-gourd cakes for other bakers to taste. Even the teahouse owner joined in, praising the pastries brought by him.

第二天，潮州糕点师傅带着一些冬瓜角回到茶馆，给其他师傅品尝，大家一致说好，甚至连茶馆老板也凑过来，称道潮州师傅带来的糕点。

"Which teahouse bakes such a good cake?" asked the owner.

"哪家茶馆做的糕点这么好吃？"老板问道。

"This cake was made by my wife from Chaozhou!" replied the baker.

"这种糕点是我那潮州老婆做的！"糕点师傅答道。

"Oh, it is the Chaozhou Wife Cake," said the owner.

"哦，是潮州老婆饼呀。"老板说。

The bakers in the teahouse began to make this kind of cakes and sell them to the customers. As a result, with the popularity of the Chaozhou style cakes, the name of the Wife Cake gradually spread far and wide.

茶馆的糕饼师便做起这种糕点卖给顾客。结果，随着潮州风味糕点流行开来，"老婆饼"的名字也逐渐广为流传。

73 The Emergence of Sugar-Coated Haws on a Bamboo Stick 冰糖葫芦的出现

Sugar-Coated Haws on a Bamboo Stick taste both sour and sweet, and this bright red fruit is favored by people old and young. Usually, a vendor uses a bamboo stick to poke pieces of fruit one by one. Then the vendor coats each piece with a thin layer of liquid candy to give it a glossy finish. Finally, the vendor inserts the ends of bunches of the haw bamboo sticks into a long-sized thick straw rod. The rod is then taken to a farmers' market or a traditional temple fair, where, among passers-by, the rod may look like a tree covered with red fruit.

冰糖葫芦酸甜可口，红艳艳的果子老少皆爱。通常，卖冰糖葫芦的会将山楂逐个串在竹棍上。然后，给红果儿涂上一层薄薄的糖液，让它看起来色泽红亮。最后，他们把一串串冰糖葫芦插在粗长的草把上，带到农贸市场或传统的庙会上叫卖，草把在行人中间就像是挂满红色硕果的树。

What are the origins of the Sugar-Coated Haws? Legend has it that it originated in the Shaoxi years of the Southern Song Dynasty. Emperor Guang Zong had a concubine whose surname was Huang. One day, Lady Huang became sick and tired. She hadn't eaten for days. The royal physicians treated her with all kinds of valuable medicines, but she still did not recover. The emperor worried all day about his beloved concubine. Finally, he had no choice but to have someone post a notice seeking medical advice.

冰糖葫芦是怎样出现的呢？相传，它始于南宋绍熙年间。光宗皇帝有一位姓黄的贵妃。一天，黄贵妃病了，虚弱疲惫，一连几天不思饮食。御医用了各种珍贵药品，却不见什么效果。皇帝见爱妃病情恶化，也整日愁眉不展。最后，他只好张榜求医。

An unknown herbalist took down the notice and went to the royal residence, where he diagnosed the disease by feeling the pulse of her wrist. Then, he said, "Boil red haws with crystal sugar and eat five to ten haws before each meal, and sickness will be gone in less than half a month."

一位无名郎中揭榜进宫，为黄贵妃把脉诊断。看后，他说："用冰糖与红果儿煎熬，每顿饭前吃五至十枚，不出半月病准见好。"

At first, no one believed him, but Huang ate the sugar-coated haws according to the herbalist's instruction. To everyone's surprise, she recovered quickly, and the emperor finally breathed a sigh of relief.

起初，没人相信他的话，但令大家大感意外的是，黄贵妃按此法服食后，竟很快就病愈了，这让皇帝松了一口气。

Haws have a number of medical benefits, such as relief from indigestion. Maybe every day Lady Huang ate all kinds of costly foods that were difficult to digest. Eating too much rich food could lead to sickness, but the haws finally made her feel better.

山楂的药用功效很多，比如能够消化积食。黄贵妃也许每天吃了各种山珍海味，难以消化。吃太多油腻食物会导致生病，但山楂最终使她感觉好多了。

Later, knowledge about the medical benefits of haws spread to the general public. The earliest way to sell sugar-coated haws was to sell them on strings, and it then gradually evolved into the present style of haws on bamboo sticks. At present, although there are a variety of haw foods on sale, people still like to eat the shiny, mouth-watering Sugar-Coated Haws on a Bamboo Stick.

后来，有关山楂药用功效的知识传到民间。冰糖葫芦最早出售的方式是串在绳上销售的，后来逐渐演变成用细竹棍串成的冰糖葫芦。目前，市面上有各种各样的山楂食品，但老百姓还是爱吃这流光溢彩、引人垂涎的冰糖葫芦串。

74 The Chinese Yam in Hot Toffee
拔丝山药

The Chinese Yam in Hot Toffee is a tasty, crispy, and sweet dessert that looks as yellow as persimmon and can be pulled out long, thin threads of sugar.

拔丝山药是脆甜爽口的甜点，呈柿黄色，能拔出又长又细的糖丝。

The Chinese Yam in Hot Toffee is a traditional Beijing dish that has a history of at least 100 years. This food is mentioned in *Brief Comments on Vegetarian Diet* written by Xue Baochen, an academician in the Imperial Academy in the Xuantong years of the Qing Dynasty. It says, "Peel yams and cut them into the shape of a circular roller; then deeply fry the yam rolls in oil, add rock candy water and remove the rolls from the heat; long threads of sugar will soon be drawn from the yam rolls. ...Local chefs in the capital city like to make this dish."

拔丝山药是北京传统名菜，少说也有百年历史。清代宣统时翰林院侍读学士薛宝辰在他写的《素食说略》中提到了此物，他在文中说道："去皮，切拐刀块，以油灼之，加入调好冰糖的水起锅，即有长丝。……京师庖人喜为之。"

There is a legend of the Chinese Yam in Hot Toffee, which is said to have originated in the Tang Dynasty.

有一则关于拔丝山药的传说，据说源于唐朝。

One day, Li Mi had dinner with Wei Zheng to discuss the method of attacking Xingyang. Li Mi wanted to make a quick attack, but Wei Zheng said nothing about the attack of Xingyang. Li Mi was very anxious, but there was nothing he could do.

一日，李密与魏征饮宴，商议攻占荥阳的办法。李密想速战速决，而魏征只字不提攻打荥阳之事。李密十分着急，可却没有其他办法。

At this time, the chef brought in a bowl of food that looked golden yellow. Immediately, Li Mi picked up the food with his chopsticks and began to eat it. "Ouch!" he cried out. The food burned his lips and blistered them.

这时，厨师端上一碗色泽金黄的食物。李密随即下筷就吃。"哎哟！"李密大叫一声。食物烫着了他的嘴唇，嘴唇随即起了血泡。

The chef quickly brought in another bowl of cold water. Wei Zheng picked up one yam roll with his chopsticks, dipped it in the cold water and then put it into his mouth. Meanwhile, he asked Li Mi to give it a try. Li Mi did the same and found it sweet, crispy, and tasty. This is said to be the origin of the Chinese Yam in Hot Toffee.

厨师立刻送上一碗凉水，魏征夹起山药往凉水里涮了涮，再放入口中。同时，他让李密试一试。李密也照此品尝，发现此物又甜又脆又好吃。据说这就是拔丝山药的来历。

While eating this food, Li Mi calmed down. Later, he and Wei Zheng carefully worked out a battle plan. As a result, Xingyang was seized, and the city commander Wang Shichong was captured alive.

李密吃着这种食物，随即冷静下来。随后，他与魏征一起制订了周密的作战计划。结果，他们攻下了荥阳，活捉守城主帅王世充。

75 The Original Lime Preserved Eggs
最初的皮蛋

Legend has it that there was a small teahouse in Wujiang of Jiangsu during the Taichang year of the Ming Dynasty. Every day, the shopkeeper of the teahouse was busy serving tea drinkers. He usually poured brewed tea into the ash by a stove after tea drinkers left.

相传，明朝泰昌年间，江苏吴江有一家小茶馆。每天，店主都忙于应酬饮茶人，在他们离开茶馆后，经常把泡过的茶叶倒入炉灰中。

The shopkeeper kept some ducks in the teahouse, and these ducks often laid their eggs in the ash, so the shopkeeper also collected the eggs there. Sometimes he would leave some eggs buried inside the ash.

店主在茶馆里养了几只鸭子，这些鸭子经常在炉灰堆里下蛋，所以店主也在那里拾鸭蛋。有时候，一些鸭蛋会被遗留在炉灰里。

One day, while cleaning away the ash and brewed tea leaves, the shopkeeper accidentally found some eggs in the ash. He thought that these eggs were uneatable as they had been covered in ash and tea leaves for some time. He broke open the shell of one of the eggs and saw something dark and glossy inside. He tried it and found that it had a unique taste.

一天，店主人在清除炉灰茶叶渣时，意外地发现了几枚埋在灰里的鸭蛋。他认为这些鸭蛋不能吃了，原因是鸭蛋被炉灰和茶叶渣覆盖了一段时间。他剥开一枚鸭蛋，看见里面黝黑光亮，他尝了尝，发现这种食物味道独特。

On the basis of this accidental discovery, people continued to improve the process of making preserved eggs. Traditional Chinese medicine believes that preserved eggs have a cooling effect and can help treat eye aching, toothache, high blood pressure, dizziness, and tinnitus.

在这次偶然发现的基础上，人们不断改进皮蛋的制作工艺。传统中医认为，皮蛋有降温作用，有助于治疗眼痛、牙痛、高血压、头晕和耳鸣。

76 The Laba Festival and the Laba Porridge 腊八节与腊八粥

The Laba Festival falls on the eighth day of the twelfth month of the Chinese lunar calendar. As is known to all, eating the Laba Porridge is a popular folk custom during the Laba Festival.

农历腊月初八日是腊八节。众所周知，喝腊八粥是腊八节期间流行的民俗。

The Laba Festival is a Buddhist holiday. In places where the ancient Han people inhabited, this day was believed to be the time when Sakyamuni attained immortality. So on that day, scriptures were chanted in monasteries, and the Laba Porridge was prepared as an offering to the Buddha.

腊八节是佛教节日。在古代汉人居住地，人们认为这一天是释迦牟尼得道成佛的日子。所以在这一天，寺庙里都要诵经，造粥供佛。

Here is a story about the Laba Porridge. Before Sakyamuni became a Buddha, he visited many mountains and rivers in India, where he met abbots and men of unusual caliber in search of the true meaning of life. When he approached a river in Northern India, hungry and hot, he was so exhausted that he fainted on the ground in a deserted area. Just then, there came a shepherdess, who fed him with her own lunch and water from a spring. The lunch was actually a mixture of leftovers from her family's kitchen over the past few days. It was mainly made up of various cereals, glutinous rice, dates, as well as wild chestnuts and fruits that she had collected on the hillside. Sakyamuni had not eaten for many days. For him, the meal was better than anything else. After the meal, he took a bath in the river and then sat under a bodhi tree to meditate. On the eighth day of the twelfth month, he attained enlightenment and became a Buddha.

关于腊八粥流传着一则故事。在释迦牟尼成佛之前，他行走印度的许多山川，走访寺院住持和高人，苦求人生真谛。当他走近印度北部一条河流时，已经筋疲力尽，又饿又热，昏倒在荒芜之地。就在这时，一位牧羊女走来，用自己的午餐和泉水喂他。午餐就是她家厨房几天来留下的剩饭，饭里主要有各种谷物、糯米、枣，还有她在山坡上采集的栗子和水果。释迦牟尼好几天没有进食了，这顿饭对他来说比什么都好。饭后，他在河里沐浴，然后在菩提树下静坐沉思，腊月初八日得道成佛。

Since then, every year on this day, monks assemble to chant scriptures, give lectures on Buddhism and eat the glutinous porridge to commemorate the day.

从那以后，每年的这一天，众僧人一起诵经，讲经，喝糯米粥，以纪念这个日子。

The custom of eating the Laba Porridge in monasteries has lasted for more than 1,000 years. By the Qing Dynasty, eating the Laba Porridge became a custom among the common people. Emperors, empresses and princesses would bestow the porridge on ministers and army officers, attendants, and palace maids. Nowadays, people still eat the Laba Porridge. According to legend, those who eat the Laba Porridge will be blessed from the Buddha.

寺院里喝腊八粥的习俗，已经延续了一千多年了。到了清朝，喝腊八粥成为民间习俗。皇帝、皇后、公主会给大臣、官员、侍从、宫女赠粥。如今，人们仍然在这个节日里喝腊八粥。据传，喝完腊八粥后，便可得到佛祖赐福。

77 The Farmer's Son and the Corn Porridge in the Imperial Kitchen 农夫的儿子与御膳房的玉米粥

According to folklore, once Emperor Kangxi of the Qing Dynasty and his bodyguards spent the whole day hunting in a mountain. When the sun was almost setting, the emperor rode back home. A moment later, a deer passed by, and the emperor immediately urged his horse to chase after it. Meanwhile, he fired a quick arrow in an attempt to stop the running deer.

相传，康熙皇帝有一天带着侍从一整天都在山里打猎。太阳快要落山时，他便策马往回走。过了一会儿，一只鹿从旁边经过，他立刻策马追赶。与此同时，他张弓搭箭，试图截住飞奔的鹿。

The emperor was soon out of sight, leaving his bodyguards far behind. As the day became darker, he went astray. He kept riding, trying to join his bodyguards.

皇帝很快就不见了踪影，把侍从远远抛在后面。天越来越暗，康熙帝迷路了。他一直策马行走，想与侍从会合。

Before long, the emperor saw a light far ahead. As he came closer, he saw that it was a farmhouse. He dismounted and walked into the house, where a gray-haired old man and his sons were about to have supper. On the dining table were slices of steamed cornbread, a large bowl of corn porridge, and a plate of braised hare with mushrooms.

走了一会儿，他见前面有灯光，近前一看，原来是一家农舍。他下了马，走进屋里，见一位白发老人和他的儿子们正准备吃晚饭。餐桌上放着几块玉米窝窝头、一大碗玉米粥和一盘香菇焖野兔。

The emperor felt hungry at the sight of the food. He said, "I am a traveler, passing through the mountain today. Can you offer me something to eat? I will pay you with silver."

康熙帝见到桌上的食物，就感到肚子饿了。他说："我是过路的，今天经过这座山。你能给我点吃的吗？我付银子。"

The locals in the mountains were known for their hospitality, so they invited him to have dinner with them.

山里人热情好客，便请他一起吃晚饭。

After dinner, the emperor said, "This is a very good meal. Who cooked it?"

饭后，康熙帝问道："这顿饭真好吃。谁做的？"

The old man said with a smile. "I have three sons. The eldest son takes charge of hunting, the second son collects firewood, and my youngest son grows vegetables and cooks at home. The dinner tonight has been cooked by my youngest son."

老人微笑道："我有三个儿子。大儿子负责打猎，二儿子拾柴，小儿子在家种菜做饭。今晚的饭菜就是小儿子做的。"

By this time, the emperor's bodyguards arrived, respectfully waiting for the emperor to depart. Judging from the way the bodyguards were dressed, the man and his three sons realized that the guest was the emperor.

正在此时，皇帝的侍从赶到了，恭敬地候着。从侍从的装束来判断，这家人才知道来客是皇帝。

"Your family lives a quiet life in the mountains. That greatly pleases me," said the emperor with a smile. He gave the old man a lot of silver and then went away.

康熙帝笑着说："你们一家平静地生活在山里，朕很高兴！"他给这位老人留下了不少银子后便离去了。

A few days later, the tasty corn porridge occurred to the emperor, so he ordered the old man's youngest son to be hired to work in the palace kitchen. His job was to cook corn porridge for the emperor. And the corn porridge became one of the snacks on the royal kitchen menu.

过了几天，康熙帝想起了可口的玉米粥，就派人雇用老汉的三儿子，让他在御膳房里专为皇帝做玉米粥，于是玉米粥便成了御膳房的小吃之一。

78 Zhu Yuanzhang and the Origin of the Fried White-Hairy Tofu 虎皮毛豆腐的起源与朱元璋

Tourists who visit Mount Huangshan in Anhui Province all

like to taste a delicious dish, namely the Fried White-Hairy Tofu. It is said that Zhu Yuanzhang, the first emperor of the Ming Dynasty, once worked hard for the rich when he was a child. In those days, he herded cattle during the day; in the middle of the night, he had to get up to grind soybeans and make tofu with long-term hired laborers. The laborers looked after him and tried not to let him do the hard work. However, their behavior angered the rich man, who then fired Zhu.

凡是来黄山的游客，都喜欢品尝一道可口的佳肴——虎皮毛豆腐。据说，明太祖朱元璋幼年曾给财主做苦工，白天放牛，半夜起来与长工们一起磨豆子，做豆腐。长工们照顾他，尽量不让他干重活，但此举却触怒了财主，随即将他辞退了。

Zhu had to live a beggar's life with younger beggars from a ruined temple. The laborers took pity on him, so every day they stole some food and fresh tofu from the rich man's home and hid them in a haystack. Then, Zhu would quietly take the food away and share it with the other younger beggars.

朱元璋只得和破庙里的小乞丐们一起过着乞丐生活。长工们可怜他，于是每天从财主家偷得一些食物和新鲜豆腐，将其藏在草垛里，然后，朱元璋便悄悄取走食物，和小乞丐们分食。

Once, Zhu and the beggars went begging in a temple fair 10 miles away from the haystack. When they came back, they found a layer of white hair on the tofu. They had no choice, but to take the white-hairy tofu back to the temple, where they fried it in a small amount of oil until it was brownishly yellow. Amazingly, the tofu exuded a delicious aroma and tasted very good.

一次，朱元璋和乞丐们到离草垛十英里远的庙会乞讨。回来后，他们发现豆腐上长出了一层白毛。他们别无选择，只得将白毛豆腐拿回庙里，用少量的油把毛豆腐煎成棕黄色。不料，豆腐散发出香气，味道也很好。

During the Zhizheng years of the Yuan Dynasty, Zhu became a leader of the anti-Yuan rebellion army. He once led an army of one hundred thousand men to Huizhou Prefecture. On the way, in order to reward his army, he specially ordered thc army cooks to make the white-hairy tofu with water from a brook, so this dish was brought to the old town and handed down from generation to generation.

元朝至正年间，朱元璋已是反元义军领袖。一次，他率领十万大军来到徽州府，途中特命随军炊厨用溪水做毛豆腐以犒赏大军，由此油煎毛豆腐传到古老的徽州府，并一代又一代地流传下来。

Later, Zhu Yuanzhang became the emperor. He ordered the palace chefs to make the Fried White-Hairy Tofu, which gradually became a must-have dish in the royal kitchen.

朱元璋即位后，便命御厨做油煎毛豆腐，这道菜逐渐成了御膳房必备菜肴。

79 Wang Zhihe and the Smelly Fermented Tofu 王致和臭豆腐

Legend has it that in the Kangxi years of the Qing Dynasty, there was a scholar named Wang Zhihe from Xianyuan of Anhui. Once, Wang went to the capital city, where he took the imperial examination but failed. After that, Wang stayed in the city, and he had to make tofu for a living because he had run out of money.

His parents taught him this skill when he was a child.

相传康熙八年，安徽仙源有位书生，名叫王致和。一次，他进京赶考，却名落孙山。之后，王致和留在京城。因为路费花光了，他不得不做豆腐谋生。当他还是小孩时，他的父母就传授过他这门手艺。

As Wang started his tofu business, he only planned to earn enough money to pay for his trip back to his hometown in Anhui. As days went by, Wang's tofu business continued in Beijing. Once, in the middle of the summer, the tofu made by Wang Zhihe was not completely sold out. Wang worried that his tofu would spoil as the temperature steadily rose throughout the day, so he cut the tofu into small cubes, sprinkled some salt and Chinese prickly ash powder on the surface, and then stored them in the inner hall.

王致和做豆腐生意最初之时，只打算赚够钱支付返回安徽老家的旅费。随着时间流逝，王致和的北京豆腐生意持续未止。一次，时值盛夏，王致和做出的豆腐没有卖完，他怕剩下的豆腐因白天气温上升而变质，便将豆腐切成小方块，在上面撒些盐和花椒粉，然后将豆腐块储存在内厅里。

A few days later, the Wangs caught an unusual smell coming from the hall. Wang Zhihe went there, and he was surprised to find that all his white-color tofu had turned into another kind. Each piece retained its original shape, but it was *qing* in color (a shade between gray and green) and gave off a strong smell. He picked one up and tasted it. "Well," he said. "I've been making tofu all my life, but I've never tasted anything like this before." Being overjoyed, Wang moved all the *qing*-colored tofu cubes out of the inner hall and put them for sale outside his shop. At the same time, he also hung up a signboard that read, "*Qing*-colored tofu cubes: smell unpleasant but taste good."

几天后，王致和和家人从厅里闻到了一股异常气味。王致和走过去，惊讶地发现白色豆腐都变成了另一种模样。每块豆腐形状依旧，但呈青色，气味强烈。他拿起一块尝了尝。"嗯，"他说，"我一生做豆腐，未尝过此物。"王致和大喜，便把所有的臭豆腐拿出内厅，放在店外叫卖。同时，他还挂起了幌子，上书"臭中有奇香的青方"。

Passers-by had never seen this new kind of tofu. Out of curiosity, some of them bought pieces to take home, and some tasted it on the spot: they all found that it tasted very good although its smell was unpleasant. The news about the sale of the *qing*-colored tofu cubes spread in the city. As a result, in less than half a day, Wang sold out all his Smelly Fermented Tofu.

路人从未见过这种豆腐。出于好奇，有人买了几块带回去，也有人现场品尝。尽管气味不雅，但他们认为味道甚佳。售卖青方豆腐的事传遍了京城，结果不到半天时间便已告罄。

One day, when Empress Dowager Cixi began her midnight meal, she suddenly had a craving for the Smelly Fermented Tofu on steamed cornbread. So one of the court eunuchs went to Wang's shop and purchased the Tofu cubes for her. From then on, the Wang's shop became famous and his tofu business was booming. Toward the end of the Qing Dynasty, the Smelly Fermented Tofu could be bought all over the capital city.

一日，慈禧太后半夜用膳，忽然想吃窝窝头就臭豆腐。于是，太监到了王致和店，为慈禧太后购买青方臭豆腐。自那以后，王致和店里的臭豆腐名声大振，其豆腐买卖也随之兴隆起来。清朝末年，王致和臭豆腐在全京城各处皆能买到。

80 Unique Pickles: Liubiju Sweet-Paste Pickles
特色小菜：六必居酱菜

Liubiju Sweet-Paste Pickles, or Liubiju Pickles, are traditional pickled vegetables in Beijing. The main products include the Sweet-Paste Muskmelon and Eight Delicacies, Sweet-Paste Black Vegetables, Chinese Artichoke in Sweet Sauce, Ginger Sprouts in Sweet Sauce, and so on.

六必居酱菜，简称"六必居"，是北京市传统小菜，主要产品有甜酱八宝瓜、甜酱黑菜、甜酱甘露、甜酱姜芽等。

Liubiju has a long history and is well known far and wide. According to historical records, Liubiju was founded by the three brothers of a Zhao family of Linfen in Shanxi during the ninth Jiajing year of the Ming Dynasty (1530). The Zhao brothers' business prospered due to their business expertise and the good location when the Liubiju stores opened. At first, Liubiju started with only two small stores and later expanded to other four separate houses, all facing the street.

六必居酱菜历史悠久，远近驰名。据史料记载，六必居始建于明朝嘉靖九年（1530），由山西临汾人赵氏三兄弟创办。六必居店开业后，赵氏兄弟的生意因他们精于买卖和优越的地理位置而蒸蒸日上。最初，六必居仅有两间小店堂，后来扩充为四间门面。

In the Jiaqing years of the Qing Dynasty, Liubiju was already well known in the capital city for its soy sauce and fermented soybeans. Later, it gradually developed into a shop which sold Liubiju Pickles, and the backyards served as processing workshops. A horizontal plaque inscribed with gilded letters hung up in front of each Liubiju store. According to legend, these letters were written by Yan Hao during the Jiajing period of the Ming Dynasty, who was of special power and influence, and his calligraphy really added much credit to Liubiju.

清朝嘉庆年间，六必居就以出售豉油而闻名京师，后来逐渐发展成为前店出售酱菜、后院做加工作坊的酱园。每家六必居店门前悬挂着金字匾额，相传系明朝嘉靖年间严嵩所书。此人权势显赫，其书法确实给六必居增色不少。

Early in the Ming and Qing dynasties, Liubiju Pickles were sold well in the market. In those days, they were indispensible at the feasts held by court nobles and officials; they were also a must for the ordinary people, who loved eating the Sweet-Paste Pickled Cucumber and the Spicy Dried Radish in Sweet Paste. Nowadays, many traditional Liubiju Pickles have become good brands and are even canned and sold abroad.

早在明清时期，六必居酱菜就十分畅销。那时候，王公贵族和朝廷官员的宴席上，少不了六必居酱菜；百姓庶民的饮食，也离不开一两碟六必居酱菜，如酱黄瓜、甜辣萝卜干等。现在，不少传统酱菜成了好品牌，甚至制成罐头，远销国外。

81 The Legend of Dried Radishes 萝卜干的传说

In China, the Dried Radish is one of the most popular dried vegetables. It is easy to be preserved and has a unique flavor. In Chaoshan area, the Dried Radish is known as *caifu* (preserved vegetables); the Shanghang Dried Radish is a specialty of Fujian; in Changzhou it is a good dish to go with liquor; in Xiaoshan it looks fairly yellow and tastes crisp, tender, and slightly spicy.

在国内，萝卜干是最受欢迎的腌菜之一，它易于保存，独具风味。萝卜干在潮汕地区称“菜脯”，上杭萝卜干是福建特产，常州萝卜干可以做下酒菜，萧山萝卜干色微黄、脆嫩、微辣。

Dried Radishes are produced in many parts of China, where many beautiful legends are derived. The following is about the legend of the Dried Radish in Shanghang.

中国许多地方出产萝卜干，各地都有关于萝卜干的许多美妙的传说。下面是一则关于上杭萝卜干的传说。

A long time ago, an immortal came to Shanghang. When he passed by Huzili area in Taiba, he felt hungry and thirsty. It was just at noon, and the sun was scorchingly hot.

很久以前，有位神仙来到上杭。他经过太拔湖子里时，感到肚饥口渴。正值中午时分，太阳火辣辣的。

So he went to a villager's house to beg for food. The villager was so friendly that he brought him tea and rice, but no vegetables. The immortal felt very strange and asked the host why there were no vegetables. "We've got a temporary shortage of vegetables," said the host. "New vegetables are not ripe yet. If I have anything now, I do have a radish."

于是，他来到一户村民家中想讨口饭吃。村民非常热情，递上了茶水，又端来米饭，却没有菜。神仙感到很奇怪，问主人怎么没菜呢？主人说：“现在蔬菜青黄不接，新种的蔬菜还没有成熟。如果说我现在有的话，确实还有一个萝卜。”

The immortal said, "The radish is good. Pull it up and cook it."

神仙说：“萝卜也好，拔出来做菜吧。”

The host looked at the immortal in bewilderment. “This radish will be kept as a seed for planting next year. If I pull it out, I won’t be able to grow radishes next year.”

主人看着神仙，一脸茫然。“这个萝卜是留作明年的种子用的。拔掉了，明年就无法再种萝卜了。”

The immortal said, “It doesn’t matter. The top half of the radish can be kept as a seed, and the bottom half can be used for cooking. Do you have any more radish seeds? If you have these seeds, you can plant them now.”

神仙说：“没关系。萝卜的上半截留作种子，下半截拿来煮吧。你还有萝卜种子吗？如果有的话，现在就可以用来播种了。”

“I have never heard of radish growing in spring,” said the host.

主人说：“我从来没听说过萝卜可以在春季生长呀。”

“That’s true,” said the immortal, pointing to the surrounding mountains. “The radish can grow everywhere as far as my eye-sight can extend. You can try it now and plant seeds here any day of the year, so that there will be radishes to eat all year round.”

“那倒是真的，”神仙指了指周围的群山说，“我目之所及的地方，都可以用来种萝卜。你现在可以试试，一年四季都可以在此地播种，这样一年四季就都有萝卜吃了。”

On hearing of that, the host was undecided whether to believe it or not. He said with a smile, “It would be very great if that were true. Today, I’m going to try to plant the seeds. However, if there are radishes all year round, we can’t eat them all. The rest of the radishes will become rotten.”

主人听了半信半疑，笑着说："如果是真的，那就太好了。我今天就去试着播种。不过，一年四季都有萝卜，哪吃得了这么多，剩下的萝卜会坏的。"

The immortal thought for a moment and said, "You can make them into dried radishes!"

神仙想了想说："可以做成萝卜干！"

"What do we do with the radishes?" asked the host.

主人问："怎么做呢？"

"It's very simple. Marinate radishes with salt and dry them in the sun. Then, put them into jars and seal them with clay paper. After eighty-one days, unseal the jars and you can eat."

"很简单，卤以白盐，而后晒干，再入瓮内，泥纸封固，时过九九，开瓮取食。"

After the immortal left, the host followed this method. Strangely enough, he planted radish seeds in April, and radishes grew in the same month. Since then, radishes have been growing all year round, so that the local people can eat fresh radishes every day and make the rest into dried radishes. The method of making dried radishes has gradually spread in Shanghang, and this kind of radishes thus becomes one of the "eight flavors" in western Fujian.

神仙走后，主人按照他说的开始干了起来。说来也奇怪，他在四月播下萝卜种子，同月就长出了果实。从那以后，萝卜一年四季都在生长，当地人每天都能吃到鲜萝卜，把剩下的就做成萝卜干。做萝卜干的方法逐渐在上杭传播开来，这种萝卜干也成为"闽西八味"之一。

82 The Original Producer of the Preserved Fuling Pickles 涪陵榨菜第一人

Fuling Pickles, sometimes referred to as Sichuan Pickles, are sold across China. The main raw materials of Fuling Pickles are green vegetable heads that grow in Fuling District. The processing technology of the pickles is unique, the flavor is appetizing, and the taste is fresh and crisp. What is more, along with the French Cornichons and German Red Cabbage, Fuling Pickles are one of the world's top three famous pickles. In addition, its traditional processing technique has been included in the second batch of the National Intangible Cultural Heritage List.

涪陵榨菜，有时也称为“四川榨菜”，在国内各地都有销售。榨菜的主要原料是生长在涪陵地区的青菜头，榨菜的加工工艺独特，风味鲜美，口感鲜脆，与法国酸黄瓜、德国甜酸甘蓝并称为世界三大名腌菜。此外，其传统制作技艺被列入第二批国家级非物质文化遗产名录。

Fuling Pickles have a history of over 100 years. Who invented Fuling Pickles? This is indeed an interesting question. According to folklore in Fuling, a man named Qiu Zhengfu lived in Zhongzhou (present-day Zhongxian County of Chongqing) in the Daoguang years of the Qing Dynasty. All day long, this man ate greasy and fatty food, which made him lose his appetite. To make matters worse, he began to lose weight.

涪陵榨菜已有百余年的历史。是谁发明的呢？这确实是一个有趣的问题。据涪陵民间传说，清朝道光年间，有个叫邱正富的人，世居忠州（今重庆忠县）。此人终日膏粱厚味，致使食欲减退，甚至身体渐渐消瘦。

One night, while he was sleeping, he dreamed of an age-old man. The man said to him, "The Baobao Vegetable Pickles from the Tianzi Monastery in Fuzhou are the best dish to be served with rice. Why not have a try?" Qiu woke up. He took the words in his dream with a pinch of salt and decided to go to the Tianzi Monastery.

一天夜晚，在他睡觉时，梦见一位老者。老者言道："涪州天子殿包包泡菜最能送食，施主何不一试？"邱正富醒来，半信半疑，决定去涪州天子殿看看。

On the ninth day of the first lunar month, Qiu arrived at Tianzi Monastery, where he burned incense and worshiped the images of Buddha. In the monastery, he had a vegetarian meal, which includes several kinds of crispy pickles. One kind of crispy pickles went well with rice. It looked green, and tasted tender and crispy.

正月初九，邱正富来到了天子殿烧香拜佛。在寺庙里，他用了斋饭，桌上放着好几种香脆的咸菜。其中一种咸菜特别送食，咸菜呈青色，吃起来又嫩又脆。

After the meal, he asked the abbot what the pickle was made from. The abbot said that these pickles were made from local *baobao* vegetables (green vegetable heads) marinated in a pickling liquid. Then he took Qiu to see the *baobao* vegetables in the monastery garden, where Qiu received a spoonful of seeds and learned how to grow and marinate the *baobao* vegetables.

饭后，他问方丈这种泡菜是用什么做成的。方丈说，泡菜是用当地包包菜腌制的。说罢，方丈便带他去寺里菜园看包包菜了。在那里，邱正富得到了一小勺种子，并学习了如何栽种和腌制包包菜。

After Qiu returned to Zhongzhou, he began to grow the *baobao* vegetables in his garden. When he harvested the *baobao* vegetables, he started to pickle them with the method he had learned in the monastery. Although his pickles were not as tender and crispy as those made in the monastery, they still tasted delicious and sharpened his appetite.

邱正富返回忠州后，就在自家菜园里种植包包菜。他收获了包包菜后，就按照在寺庙学的方法腌制。虽然腌制的泡菜不及天子殿的嫩脆，但还是好吃，能增加食欲。

Therefore, Qiu saved some seeds, and sowed them the following year. But strangely, these seeds did not sprout. Once again, he asked for some seeds of the *baobao* vegetables from the Tianzi Monastery. Still strangely enough, the first year was a good harvest, but the second year again did not see the *baobao* vegetables coming out.

于是，邱正富留了一些种子，并在次年播种。但奇怪的是，次年播下的种子却不长包包菜。于是，他再次从天子殿要来了种子。仍令人感到不可思议的是，第一年虽获得了丰收，但次年还是长不出包包菜。

It seemed hard to believe. So Qiu went to Fuzhou, where he bought a piece of land by the Ximo Creek on the east side of the Tianzi Monastery. At the same time, his family moved to Fuzhou, too. Since then, he had had enough *baobao* vegetables to make pickles every year. He lived to the age of 93 and died without any illness. Later, the descendants of the Qiu family invented preserved pickles on the basis of the local people's processing of salted *baobao* vegetables.

这似乎不可思议。于是，邱正富来到涪州，在天子殿以东的洗墨溪买下一块地。同时，举家迁到涪州。从那以后，邱正富年年有包包菜做泡菜了。他活到93岁，无疾而终。后来，邱氏后人在当地人腌制的包包咸菜的基础上发明了榨菜。

In 1939, Zhang Xiaomei said in *The Reference Material of Sichuan Economics: Preserved Pickles*, "Qiu Shou'an, a native of Fuling, had a well-off family. At ordinary times, he made pickles in many jars at home for his family to use. In the late Xuantong years, Qiu went to Yihan, carrying more than ten pickle jars to give to his friends and relatives. The pickles made by him were well received, so Qiu quietly returned to Sichuan, where he engaged in the monopoly business of shipping pickles out of the province."

1939年，张肖梅在《四川经济参考资料：榨菜》中写道："涪陵人邱寿安，家世小康，平时自制多坛家用。邱君于宣统末年赴宜汉，随带十余坛送亲友，获得赞美，遂秘密返川经营，专运省外。"

According to *The Sequel to the Fuling Chronicle* published in 1928, "The Qiu family recently sold Fuling Pickles to Shanghai, and his business even spread overseas. The *baobao* vegetables grow widely in the rural areas." Fuling Pickles have become famous ever since.

据1928年出版的《涪陵县续修涪州志》载："近邱氏贩榨菜至上海，行销及海外，乡间多种之。"涪陵榨菜自此享有盛誉。

83 Stories About Vinegar
醋的故事

Vinegar was invented in China a long time ago. It is said that

3,500 years ago, King Zhou, the last king of the Shang Dynasty, gouged Bigan's heart to decoct it with other herbs to treat the ailing concubine Daji. However, in order to enhance the efficacy of the decoction, an alcoholic beverage needed to be added as the ingredient. At that time, as *fenjiu* in Shanxi was a well-known alcohol, the king ordered workmen from the *fenjiu* workshop to carry the liquor to the capital of the Shang Dynasty.

很久以前，中国就发明了醋。据说3,500年前，商朝纣王挖比干之心，准备与其他草药煎熬，给妃子妲己治病。然而，为了提高汤剂的药效，需要加入酒浆作为药引。当时，山西汾酒是知名白酒，纣王便下令汾酒作坊的伙计把酒送到商朝都城。

The workmen hired porters to carry liquor buckets to the capital. It was a long journey that started in the middle of summer, and all the workmen and porters suffered from heatstroke. As the workers sat resting by the side of the road, they opened the buckets to see if the liquor still tasted all right.

伙计们雇了挑夫把酒桶抬往都城。这是一次始于仲夏的长途旅程，所有的伙计和挑夫都中暑了。伙计们坐在路边休息，他们打开酒桶，查看酒味变了没有。

Unexpectedly, the liquor in the buckets turned sour. The workmen and porters were frightened, for they knew that if they presented the sour liquor to the king in the capital, they would be beheaded. Hopelessly, they decided to commit suicide by drinking all the sour liquor.

出乎意料的是，酒桶的酒变酸了。伙计们和挑夫惊慌不已，心想如果把这样的酒献给京城纣王，会遭斩首的。无奈之下，他们决定喝光变酸的酒自杀。

Two hours later, they were still alive. In addition, their symptoms of heatstroke disappeared, and they all felt refreshed on the journey. Instead of continuing on to the capital, they fled back to their home in the countryside, where they succeeded in distilling the sour liquor. They found that the sour liquid could make food tasty and stimulate the appetite. Then, in the same process, they distilled more of this liquid and sold it to their neighbors. As a result, the sour liquid became popular with many people far and wide.

两小时后，他们竟还活着。此外，中暑症状消失了，而且在旅途中他们都感到神清气爽。他们没有继续前往都城，而是逃回乡下老家，在那里成功地酿出了酸味液体。他们发现这种酸液会使食物味好可口，可以促进食欲，于是，他们依法酿制更多的这种液体，售卖给街坊四邻。结果，这种酸液远近闻名，受到欢迎。

Prior to the reign of Emperor Wen Di of the Han Dynasty, there was no such thing as *cu* (vinegar). The flavoring liquid that produced the sour taste was called *xi*. Empress Dowager Bo, a native of Shanxi, felt uncomfortable whenever she heard the name of *laoxi* (old vinegar). When Emperor Wen Di learned of this, he ordered his officials to think of a good name to replace it. One official thought for a moment and said, "Today is the 21st day of the 12th lunar month (腊月) in the Year of Guiyou (癸酉). Why don't we just call it *cu* (醋, vinegar)?" The emperor praised it repeatedly. He wrote down the word *cu* and pasted it on a *xi* container. Since then, the sour-taste liquid has been known as *cu* (vinegar).

汉文帝以前，根本没有醋这个叫法，产生酸味的调味液称之为"醯"。薄太后是晋人，一听到"老醯"这个名字，心里就不舒服。因醯是用于盛酸味液体的器皿，故酸液便以"醯"记之。薄太后是山西人，一听到"老醯"这个名字，心里就不舒服。汉文帝知道此事后，便吩咐臣子们想个好名字来取代“醯”。一名大臣想了想，道：“今天是癸酉年腊月二十一日，不如叫‘醋’吧。”汉文帝连连称赞，亲笔书写了“醋”字，贴在盛“醯”的器皿上。自此以后，这种酸味液体便被称为“醋”了。

In ancient times, vinegar was a popular condiment and it was considered as one of the seven daily necessities of life. Therefore, there were several stories about vinegar drinking. One story tells how vinegar drinking became a synonym for "jealousy." It is said that in order to win the favor of his subordinates, Emperor Tai Zong of the Tang Dynasty decided to present several beautiful women as concubines to prime minister Fang Xuanling. When Fang's wife heard of this, she firmly refused the emperor's gift. The emperor summoned Fang's wife and said to her, "If you allow your husband to take concubines, you will go on living a quiet life, otherwise you will have to drink the poisoned wine and die."

在古代，醋是比较普及的调味品，是开门七件事之一，由此延伸出若干吃醋的故事。其中一则讲述了“吃醋”是怎样成为“忌妒”的同义词的。据说，唐太宗为了笼络人心，准备赐几名美女给宰相房玄龄做妾。房玄龄之妻听说后，坚决拒绝皇帝的赏赐。唐太宗叫来房玄龄的夫人，对她说道：“如果你同意你丈夫纳妾，你就会过着平静的生活；若不同意，那就饮下此杯毒酒而亡吧。”

Upon hearing this, Fang's wife took a cup full of "the poisoned wine" from a tray held by an attendant of the emperor. She drank it down at once. However, it turned out that the cup was actually filled with vinegar but not poisoned wine. From then on, the emperor no longer sent beautiful women to Fang. This story became so widely known that people began to use "vinegar drinking" as a metaphor for "jealousy."

房玄龄之妻闻听此话，就从侍从端着的盘子上拿起一杯"毒酒"一饮而尽。然而，原来杯里装的是醋，而不是毒酒。从此，唐太宗不再送美女给房玄龄了。此事流传甚广，人们便用"吃醋"来比喻"忌妒"一词。

84 Arrival of Chili Pepper in China 辣椒进入中国

Chili pepper is native to Mexico, Central America, and parts of South America. It is called capsicum pepper. Before the arrival of Spaniards, the Indians in Peru and Guatemala used capsicum pepper to treat stomach pains and other ailments. The Spanish found it in the New World and brought it back to Europe.

辣椒原产于墨西哥、中美洲以及南美洲部分地区。西班牙人到来之前，秘鲁和危地马拉的印第安人用辣椒治疗胃痛和其他疾病。西班牙人在新大陆发现了辣椒，并将此物带回了欧洲。

Around the end of the 17th century, it was introduced into China. The locals in Chaozhou area of Guangdong call chili pepper *fanjiao*, which means "foreign pepper." It is unclear how exactly chili pepper was introduced into China, although there are several different stories. It might have been brought to China along China's Ancient Northwestern Silk Route, or even along the southeast coast into Guangdong and Guangxi. According to the latest research, chili pepper was probably first introduced to Jiangsu, Zhejiang, Guangdong, and Guangxi areas. Gradually, it spread to Guizhou, Hunan, Sichuan, and other places.

大约17世纪末，辣椒被引进中国。广东潮州地区的人们称辣椒为"番椒"，意指"外国辣椒"。辣椒是怎样传入中国的呢？有一种说法是，辣椒可能是通过西北丝绸之路传入中国的，也有人说辣椒可能是沿东南沿海一带传入广东和广西的。根据最新研究，辣椒最初可能被引进到江苏、浙江、广东和广西地区，然后渐渐传入贵州、湖南、四川等地。

At the beginning, chili pepper was used as an ornamental plant rather than consumption food, but in the early Qing Dynasty, the locals in Guizhou and its surrounding areas began eating chili pepper. In the Kangxi years, due to a shortage of salt in Guizhou, people used chili pepper instead of salt.

一开始，辣椒只是作为一种观赏植物，而不是当成食物。但在清初，贵州及周边地区的当地人开始食用辣椒。康熙年间，贵州缺盐，人们便用辣椒来替代。

In the Jiaqing years, chili pepper was not eaten in Hunan. However, toward the end of the Qing Dynasty, it became popular there. According to historical records, people in Hunan at that time usually "disliked eating food if the dishes had no chili pepper or mustard, and most soups were added with them."

嘉庆年间，湖南尚无食用辣椒。然而接近清末年间，辣椒在当地流行起来。据历史记载，当时湖南人"无椒芥不下箸也，汤则多有之"。

The earliest time that some local peasants in Sichuan began to grow and eat chili pepper was probably during the Jiaqing period of the Qing Dynasty. Gradually, it became a common vegetable in western Sichuan. Usually, people called chili pepper "*haijiao*" (sea pepper), indicating that they came from overseas countries.

四川农民最早开始种植食用辣椒的时间可能是在清朝嘉庆时期。

渐渐地，辣椒在川西地区成了大众化的蔬菜。人们通常称辣椒为“海椒”，这说明此物是从海外传入的。

Toward the end of the Qing Dynasty, peasants grew chili pepper all over Sichuan, and restaurants used it to prepare spicy dishes. At present, chili pepper grows all year round in Chengdu. Vegetable markets usually provide green pepper in May, red pepper in June, and large, lantern-shaped red pepper in June and July. Chili pepper is not only an important vegetable, but also an essential seasoning in various dishes. Dishes with chili pepper have a pungent and spicy flavor, a fish-tasted flavor, or other flavors.

将近清朝末年，四川各地农民都在种植辣椒，餐馆亦用此物烹制辣味菜肴。目前，成都四季生长辣椒。通常，五月蔬菜市场上有青椒，六月有红椒，六月到七月有灯笼大红椒。辣椒不仅是重要蔬菜，也是各种菜肴必不可少的佐料，用辣椒做的菜肴有麻辣味的、鱼香味的，也有其他风味的。

85 Interesting Anecdotes About Radishes
萝卜的趣闻轶事

A radish tastes sweet, crispy, and juicy. Since ancient times, there have been many interesting stories about radishes.

萝卜味甜、脆、多汁。自古以来，就有许多关于萝卜的趣闻轶事。

During the Three Kingdoms Period, the allied forces led by Liu Bei and Sun Quan defeated Cao Cao and his troops in the Battle of the Red Cliff. Shortly after the end of the battle, Cao Cao led his men to fight their way out along the Huarong Pass. Thousands of his men could go no further because of the hot weather, hunger, and thirst. Just then, they happened to pass by a large field of radishes, so they rushed into the field where they pulled the radishes out to satisfy their hunger. Later, the field was known as "Cao Cao's Lucky Field."

三国时期，赤壁之战，孙刘联军击败曹操大军。战后不久，曹操率领部下从华容道夺路而逃。由于天气炎热，几万大军又饥又渴，实在走不动了。就在此时，将士们碰巧经过大片萝卜地，便冲进地里拔起萝卜充饥。后来，此地被称为“救曹田”。

More than 1,300 years ago, under the rule of Wu Zetian, the only empress in ancient China, there were almost no wars, and people lived in peace.

1,300多年前，在中国古代唯一的女皇武则天的统治下，天下太平，少有战争。

Once in autumn, near the East Gate of Luoyang, there was a vegetable patch where a huge radish that was about one meter long grew. It was green on the top and white on the bottom. Local peasants regarded it as a rare vegetable and presented it to the royal palace.

一年秋天，在洛阳东关菜地长出了一个特大的萝卜，大约三尺长，上青下白，农民视为奇物，将其献入宫廷。

The empress was very happy when the huge radish was displayed in the palace. She ordered her royal chefs to cook it. Although the chefs knew that it was almost impossible to make a delicious radish dish, they didn't give up and worked hard, hoping to content the empress.

特大萝卜在宫中展示，女皇大悦，传旨御厨用萝卜烹饪。尽管厨师们知道要用萝卜做出好菜几乎是不可能的，但他们没有放弃，一直忙活着，期望能让女皇满意。

They shredded the radish and cooked it with other delicacies from land and sea. The empress ate the stewed radish and drank the broth. She lavished praise on the dish for its unique taste, saying it was just like the Eatable Nest of Cliff Swallows.

他们把萝卜切成细丝，与山珍海味一起烹制。女皇吃了炖煮的萝卜，喝了汤，对这道菜的独特味道赞不绝口，夸它大有燕窝风味。

From then on, noble families began to treat their guests with radishes as one of the main ingredients. And this dish eaten by the empress became ambrosia at banquets or dinner parties.

从此，贵族家庭都把萝卜作为一种主要食材招待客人，而女皇吃的这道菜成了宴会上的珍馐美味。

86 Emperor Qianlong and Yangchun Noodles 阳春面与乾隆皇帝

Yangchun Noodles, also known as Noodles in Clear Soup, are one of the most distinctive wheaten foods in Suzhou.

阳春面，又称清汤面，是苏州最具特色的面食之一。

According to legend, Emperor Qianlong once made a tour in the south. When he arrived in Huai'an, it was the third lunar month of the spring. There, he got rid of his entourage and the local officials, allowing only one official from the Minister of Rites to accompany him to wander around the city. Finally, they came to a noodles stall, where they sat down at the table to get something to eat.

传说乾隆皇帝下江南，他到达淮安时，正值阳春三月。乾隆帝摆脱了随从和当地官员，只让礼部一名官员陪同他在淮安城转悠。最后，他们来到面摊前，坐下来，要吃点东西。

After a while, the stall vendor brought them two bowls of noodles. Each noodle piece in the bowls had smooth surface and was pleasing to the eye. In addition, golden oily drops and chopped scallions were sprinkled on the clear noodle soup, giving off an aromatic odor.

过了一会儿，摊主给他们端来两碗面条，每根面条光面爽目。此外，金黄的油花和碎葱花洒在淡酱色面汤上，散发出扑鼻的香味。

When the emperor finished eating, he asked, "What is the name of the noodles?"

乾隆帝吃完后，问道："这种面条叫什么名字？"

The stall vendor said, "It didn't have a name yet."

摊主说："还没有名字。"

"What, such delicious noodles have no name? It's incredible!" the emperor said. He thought for a moment and said again, "Now, it is Yangchun (the third lunar month in spring), why not call it Yangchun Noodles?"

"这么好吃的面条居然没有名字？这令人难以置信！"乾隆帝说道。他想了想，又说道："现在是阳春三月，就叫'阳春面'吧。"

Upon hearing this, the official who accompanied him immediately asked somebody else to take out the writing brush, ink stick, paper, and ink-stone, and kindly invited the emperor to write down the characters “阳春面” (Yangchun Noodles).

那名陪同官员听到这个建议，立刻唤人拿出笔墨纸砚，恳请皇帝赐名“阳春面”。

87 Sichuan Fermented Bean Curd, a Delicacy in Sichuan and Chongqing
川渝美食：四川豆腐乳

Fermented bean curd is a popular side dish that can be served well with rice and other main courses.

豆腐乳开胃又下饭，是一种很受欢迎的食品。

In the Tang Dynasty, according to legend, there was a simple peasant who lived on Pingdu Mountain in today's Fengdu County of Chongqing. In addition to farming, he sold some fresh bean curd on the streets to make ends meet.

传说在唐朝，有一个淳朴的农民，住在当今重庆丰都县的平都山上。除了务农，他还在街上卖些鲜豆腐以维持生计。

One day, despite the hot weather, the peasant loaded bean curd in a basket, carried the basket on his back and walked down the mountain. he felt tired midway, so he took off the load and had a rest.

一天，天气炎热，农夫把豆腐装进篮子后，背起篮子，下山了。途中，他累了，便卸下篮子小憩。

While resting, the peasant heard the sound of chess playing. He turned around and saw two old men playing Chinese chess under a big tree. They looked like immortals with white hair and ruddy cheeks. The peasant walked up to them. There were few pieces left on their chessboard, but the two sides were evenly matched.

休息时，农夫听到了弈棋声。他转过身，只见两位老翁在大树下对弈。老翁鹤发童颜，活像神仙。农夫走去，棋盘上的棋子所剩无几，但双方依然不分胜负。

After a while, he remembered that he had to go down the mountain to sell his bean curd. By then, he was unaware that he had entered the place: "Only seven days one has been in the cave, while outside thousands of years have passed." When he turned around and found his bean curd all moldy, he felt at a loss what to do with the moldy bean curd because it was vital to his family's livelihood.

过了一会儿，他想起自己还得下山去卖豆腐。这时，他并不知道自己进入了那个"洞中方七日，世上已千年"的地方。他转过身，只见豆腐全发霉了，不知道该怎么办才好，因为豆腐对他的家庭生计至关重要。

Seeing this, the two old men comforted him by saying that if he added some salt, wine, and spices to the moldy bean curd, it would taste very good. So the peasant returned home and started to process the bean curd as suggested by the old men. As expected, the bean curd with salt, wine, and spices smelt good and was tasty. Then he loaded the processed bean curd in his basket, carried his load down the mountain and out into the streets, where the locals rushed to buy his processed bean curd. At that time, no one knew that the processed bean curd had been fermented with salt, wine, and spices. Later, the story of the old immortals advising the peasant to produce Fermented Bean Curd was widespread in the region.

见此状况，两位老翁安慰农夫说，给发霉的豆腐加些盐、酒和香料，豆腐就会美味可口。于是，农夫回到家，按照老翁的办法加工豆腐。果然，加了盐、酒和香料的豆腐既香又好吃，农夫随即把做好的豆腐装进篮子，背下山，走街串巷叫卖，当地人争相购买。那时，没有人知道这种豆腐是放入盐、酒和香料发酵而成的。后来，仙翁指点农民制作豆腐乳的故事在该地区广为流传。

88 Zhao Kuangyin and Bread Pieces Soaked in Mutton Soup 羊肉泡馍与赵匡胤

Bread Pieces Soaked in Mutton Soup are good traditional fare in the Central Shaanxi. According to legend, it has evolved from the ancient "beef and sheep soup" with a history of more than 2,000 years old. However, the most popular story of this dish is related to Zhao Kuangyin, the first emperor of the Song Dynasty.

羊肉泡馍是关中一道传统风味佳肴。传说，羊肉泡馍是由古代的"牛羊羹"演化而来的，具有两千多年的历史。然而，最流行的羊肉泡馍故事与宋朝开国皇帝赵匡胤有关系。

It is said that at the end of the Five Dynasties, Zhao was penniless and poor. One day, when he was walking aimlessly along a street in Chang'an, he felt very hungry and went to a bread bakery to beg something to eat. The shopkeeper took pity on him and gave him two slices of baked bread. The bread was dry and hard to bite because it was leftovers from a few days earlier.

据说，五代末年，赵匡胤穷困潦倒。一日，当他在长安的大街上游荡时，感到饥肠辘辘，便到了一家烧饼铺讨吃的。店主可怜他，给他两块烧饼。烧饼是几天前剩下的，干硬咬不动。

At this time, a heady delicious smell of meat came. Not far

away was a butcher's store, where mutton was being cooked. Zhao went there and got a bowl of mutton soup from the store. Then he broke the dry baked bread into small pieces and soaked them into the soup. Unexpectedly, the soup softened the small pieces, and at the same time its flavor permeated through them. He felt comfortably full after eating the bread and drinking the soup.

这时，一股肉香扑鼻而来。不远处，有一家正在煮羊肉的肉铺。于是，赵匡胤去讨了一碗羊肉汤，然后把干硬的烧饼掰成小块，泡进汤里。没想到，肉汤泡软了烧饼，同时汤的香味也渗入烧饼里，这让赵匡胤吃了烧饼喝完汤后感觉非常舒畅。

A few years later, Zhao came to power and became the first emperor of the Song Dynasty.

几年后，赵匡胤掌权了，成为宋朝开国皇帝。

One day, the bowl of Bread Pieces Soaked in Mutton Soup occurred to him. Immediately, he ordered an imperial chef to cook it. However, he found that the taste from the imperial kitchen was different from that of the old days.

一天，他想起了那碗羊肉泡馍，便立即命御厨做来。然而，他发现御厨做的和当年的味道就是不一样。

Zhao later went out on a tour of inspection. When he arrived in Chang'an, he revisited the street he had walked aimlessly along before. Right there, the long-lost smell of meat came back again.

后来，赵匡胤出巡，到了长安。他重游了当年曾游荡过的那条街，在那里又闻到了久违的肉香。

Well, the smell whetted his appetite. He got off his imperial carriage and went straight to the butcher's, where he immediately asked the store owner to make a bowl of Bread Pieces Soaked in Mutton Soup.

这一下，赵匡胤食欲顿起，他下了御辇，直奔肉铺，让店主马上做一碗羊肉泡馍。

The emperor's visit pleasantly surprised the shop owner. Since all the bread bakeries down the street were closed, he arranged his wife to bake bread.

皇上来访让店主又惊又喜。由于街上所有的烧饼铺都关门了，店主就让妻子烙饼。

He then broke the freshly-baked bread into small pieces, for he was afraid that the emperor would not like the unleavened bread. Then he poured mutton soup over the small pieces and cooked the soup to a boil. Finally, he topped slices of mutton on the soup, and added to the soup more with spinach, fine vermicelli, and chopped scallions, as well as a few drops of pepper oil.

不久，店主把刚烙好的饼掰成小块，他担心皇帝不喜欢吃死面饼，便浇上羊肉汤煮沸，最后在汤上放了羊肉片，又在汤里放入菠菜、粉丝、葱花，还有几滴花椒油。

And Zhao was served a steaming bowl of Bread Pieces Soaked in Mutton Soup. He smelt the soup. That delectable smell instantly reminded him of the old days. Under the rapt gaze of his courtiers and guards, the emperor ate it to his heart's content. After eating, he felt happy and rewarded the store owner immediately.

一碗热气腾腾的羊肉泡馍端到赵匡胤面前。他闻了闻，这香味立刻让他想起了过去的日子。在朝臣和侍卫们目不转睛的注视下，皇帝吃得津津有味。吃完后，他感到惬意，当即赏赐了店主。

The story of the emperor eating Bread Pieces Soaked in Mutton Soup in Chang'an spread far and wide overnight, and more and more people came to the store to eat. And the owner made use of this opportunity and changed the name of the butcher's to the Restaurant of Bread Pieces Soaked in Mutton Soup. In addition, as more people came to eat, the store owner was too busy to break bread, so those who came to eat had to break bread by themselves, thus injecting a lot of fun into this snack.

一夜之间，皇帝在长安城吃羊肉泡馍的事情传遍了四方，越来越多的人来到这家店里吃羊肉泡馍，店主也趁机把店名改成了“羊肉泡馍馆”。由于来吃的人越来越多，店主忙得很，无暇掰馍，所以谁吃谁就自己掰，由此为这道小吃增添了许多情趣。

附录
Appendix

中国历史年代简表*
A Brief Chronology of Chinese History

朝代 Dynasties	起讫 Date
夏 Xia Dynasty	c. 2070 – 1600 B.C.
商 Shang Dynasty	1600 – 1046 B.C.
周 Zhou Dynasty	
西周 Western Zhou Dynasty	1046 – 771 B.C.
东周 Eastern Zhou Dynasty	770 – 256 B.C.
春秋时代 Spring and Autumn Period	770 – 476 B.C.
战国时代 Warring States Period	475 – 221 B.C.
秦 Qin Dynasty	221 – 206 B.C.
汉 Han Dynasty	
西汉 Western Han Dynasty	206 B.C. – 25 A.D.
文帝 Wen Di, emperor	179 – 157 B.C.
武帝 Wu Di, emperor	140 – 87 B.C.
东汉 Eastern Han Dynasty	25 – 220
三国 Three Kingdoms	
魏 Kingdom of Wei	220 – 265
蜀 Kingdom of Shu	221 – 263
吴 Kingdom of Wu	222 – 280

（待续）

* 本简表仅含正文中出现的朝代和时期，供读者对照参考。

（续表）

朝代 Dynasties	起讫 Date
晋 Jin Dynasty	
西晋 Western Jin Dynasty	265 – 317
永熙 Yongxi year	290
东晋 Eastern Jin Dynasty	317 – 420
南北朝 Southern and Northern Dynasties	
南朝 Southern Dynasties	
宋 Song Dynasty	420 – 479
齐 Qi Dynasty	479 – 502
梁 Liang Dynasty	502 – 557
陈 Chen Dynasty	557 – 589
北朝 Northern Dynasties	
北魏 Northern Wei Dynasty	386 – 534
东魏 Eastern Wei Dynasty	534 – 550
北齐 Northern Qi Dynasty	550 – 577
西魏 Western Wei Dynasty	535 – 556
北周 Northern Zhou Dynasty	557 – 581
隋 Sui Dynasty	581 – 618
炀帝 Yang Di, emperor	605 – 617
唐 Tang Dynasty	618 – 907
太宗 Tai Zong, emperor	627 – 649
五代 Five Dynasties	
后梁 Later Liang Dynasty	907 – 923
后唐 Later Tang Dynasty	923 – 936
后晋 Later Jin Dynasty	936 – 947
后汉 Later Han Dynasty	947 – 950
后周 Later Zhou Dynasty	951 – 960
宋 Song Dynasty	
北宋 Northern Song Dynasty	960 – 1127
神宗 Shen Zong, emperor	1068 – 1085
南宋 Southern Song Dynasty	1127 – 1279

（待续）

（续表）

朝代 Dynasties	起讫 Date
建炎 Jianyan years（高宗 Gao Zong, emperor）	1127 – 1130
绍兴 Shaoxing years（高宗 Gao Zong, emperor）	1131 – 1162
绍熙 Shaoxi years	1190 – 1194
理宗 Li Zong, emperor	1225 – 1264
辽 Liao Dynasty	907 – 1125
金 Jin Dynasty	1115 – 1234
元 Yuan Dynasty	1206 – 1368
至正 Zhizheng years	1341 – 1368
明 Ming Dynasty	1368 – 1644
洪武 Hongwu years	1368 –1398
正德 Zhengde years	1506 – 1521
嘉靖 Jiajing years	1522 – 1566
泰昌 Taichang year	1620
清 Qing Dynasty	1616 – 1911
顺治 Shunzhi years	1644 – 1661
康熙 Kangxi years	1662 – 1722
乾隆 Qianlong years	1736 – 1795
嘉庆 Jiaqing years	1796 – 1820
道光 Daoguang years	1821 – 1850
咸丰 Xianfeng years	1851 – 1861
同治 Tongzhi years	1862 – 1874
光绪 Guangxu years	1875 – 1908
宣统 Xuantong years	1909 – 1911
中华民国 Republic of China	1912 – 1949

中华人民共和国1949年10月1日成立

The People's Repubic of China, founded on October 1, 1949

参考文献
References

Bauer, Beth. (1987) *Enjoy China More*. Cain-Lockhart Press, Issaquah, Washington.

De Mente, Boye. (1989) *Chinese Etiquette and Ethics in Business*. NTC Business Books, a division of NTC Publishing Group, Illinois.

Harper, Damian, Marie Cambon, Bradley Mayhew, Katja Gaskell, Korina Miller, Thomas Huhti & Mielikki Org. (2002) *China* 中国 (Eighth Edition). Lonely Planet Publications, Oakland.

Hu Wenzhong & Cornelius Grove. (1999) *Encountering the Chinese: A Guide for Americans* (Second Edition). Intercultural Press, INC, Maine.

Kaplan, Fredric, Julian Soblin & Arne de Keijzer. (1988) *China Guidebook* (Ninth Edition). Eurasia Press, New Jersey.

Wang Yanrong & Yu Shenquan. (1990) *Chinese Cooking* 怎样做中国菜. Morning Glory Publishers, a Subsidiary of China International Book Trading Corporation, Beijing.

陈达，(2003)《英汉互译理论与实践》，成都：巴蜀书社。

成都市地方志编纂委员会办公室，(2019)《成都精览》，*An Essential Survey of Chengdu*，陈达、杨存友、李学芹、龚小萍、郭志军译，北京：旅游教育出版社。

龚小萍、陈达、许媛鸿，(2014)《中国翻译理论构建中的主体性困境及其对策》，北京：外语教学与研究出版社。

齐星，（1988）《中国传统节日民俗》，北京：外文出版社。

王建辉、易学金，（1991）《中国文化知识精华》，武汉：湖北人民出版社。

杨天庆，（2007）《沿途导游掌中宝》（英语导游文化讲解资料库），北京：旅游教育出版社。

杨天庆，（2010）《沿途导游妙锦囊》（英语导游文化讲解资料库），北京：旅游教育出版社。

杨天庆，（2013）《和老外聊文化中国》（升级版），成都：天地出版社。

周沙尘，（1987）《古今北京》（第二版），北京：新世界出版社。